KNOWLEDGE

INTO ACTION:

IMPROVING THE

NATION'S USE

OF THE SOCIAL

SCIENCES

Report of the Special Commission on the
Social Sciences of the National Science Board

NATIONAL SCIENCE FOUNDATION
1969

LETTER OF TRANSMITTAL

New York, New York
May 15, 1969

Dear Dr. Handler:

I have the honor to transmit herewith the report of the Special Commission on the Social Sciences, established by the National Science Board in 1968.

Orville G. Brim, Jr.
*Chairman, Special Commission on
the Social Sciences*

Chairman, National Science Board

NATIONAL SCIENCE BOARD

FOREWORD

The aftermath of World War II left our nation with a markedly enlarged capability for research in the natural sciences and engineering and an enhanced appreciation of the values of such research for American society. Although the development of a given scientific field must proceed at its own pace, once such a field was ripe relatively little time was lost in the applied research and development activities necessary to translate fundamental understanding into useful application. This scientific capability was deliberately expanded over the next two decades and the consequences are evident everywhere in the health, security, and economy of the American people. Regrettably, during this period there occurred a much lesser strengthening and growth of research in the social sciences. Few mechanisms for translation of social scientific understanding into societal benefit have been institutionalized so as to assure this process.

In some degree, the most painful problems of our loosely structured society are the immediate or indirect consequence of the rapid success of technological endeavors. In other instances, ancient wrongs appear intolerable to a nation wealthy beyond the dreams of any previous age. Our social and domestic problems overwhelm the historical mechanisms erected at community, state, and national levels. With the passage of time, these problems appear ever more acute while, increasingly, it is evident that approaches to their solution should be undertaken only in the light of the most sophisticated social scientific understanding and the advice of the most knowledgeable professionals.

The Special Commission on the Social Sciences was brought into being by the National Science Board in the hope that its distinguished membership could provide guidance and a sense of direction to the many diverse groups concerned with the understanding and insights of the social sciences and their application to the problems of American society. The Board welcomes this report, a synthesis of the deliberations of this knowledgeable and concerned Commission.

The report is offered and commended to all of those in Government, universities, foundations, and community action groups

vii

whose concerted efforts will be required if American society is to achieve its potential, the fulfillment of the American dream.

Philip Handler
Chairman
National Science Board

ACKNOWLEDGMENTS

The Special Commission gratefully acknowledges the consultation and advice of many social scientists, members of the professions, and persons in business and in government. This report is in very large measure a collaborative effort of those in the nation concerned with the utilization of the social sciences; their response to the requests of the Special Commission has been notably cooperative and helpful. The following have contributed to one or more sections: Ivar Berg, Albert D. Biderman, Albert Cherns, John A. Clausen, Henry David, W. Phillips Davison, John T. Dunlop, Abbott L. Ferriss, David A. Goslin, Fred Iklé, Morris Janowitz, Alfred J. Kahn, Seymour M. Lipset, Gene M. Lyons, S. M. Miller, Wilbert E. Moore, Harold Orlans, James M. Oswald, Eli A. Rubinstein, Eleanor Bernert Sheldon, Herbert A. Simon, M. Brewster Smith, Richard C. Snyder, Norman W. Storer, Robert D. Vinter, Edmund H. Volkart, Roland L. Warren, and Stanton Wheeler. Felicity Skidmore and Irene Glynn have contributed much appreciated editorial advice. The final report is, of course, the responsibility only of the Commission.

SUMMARY OF MAJOR RECOMMENDATIONS

The Special Commission on the Social Sciences, established by the National Science Board in 1968, was charged with making recommendations for increasing the useful application of the social sciences in the solution of contemporary social problems. The Commission believes the nation is missing crucial opportunities to utilize fully the best of social science knowledge and skills in the formation, evaluation, and execution of policies for achieving desired social goals.

The Commission's recommendations are focused on: (1) the revitalization of existing organizations, (2) the establishment of new social institutions, and (3) the development of better channels for the flow of social science resources into American life. To implement certain of the recommendations requires little or no increase in expenditures at the community or federal level, but implementation of other recommendations will require substantial additional funds.

Our survey of the present state of utilization of the social sciences demonstrates that they have developed acceptable scientific procedures for collection of valid information on the problems they confront. They have substantially increased their scientific body of knowledge over the past decades. They have also developed excellent methods of analysis and evaluation for testing theoretical and practical propositions. Even where great gaps of knowledge remain, as they undoubtedly do, the social scientists' experience can offer valuable intuitive understanding and special insight.

Because of these gaps, and because of the complexity of the social world, social scientists are not always prepared to formulate appropriate hypotheses for testing. But this does not imply that the social sciences cannot help the nation solve its social problems. We are convinced, indeed, that they can contribute to solving the nation's problems if full advantage is taken of their strengths.

Social scientists manifestly must be consulted in the collection of relevant information, and in evaluating social policies already in existence; their knowledge and informed intelligence should also be sought out before new social programs are instituted. Even where they may not know how to design substantially better programs than those presently responsible for such programs, their professional knowledge enables them to detect and avoid pitfalls in social program design—particularly those pitfalls into which nontrained planners are enticed by the charms of conventional wisdom.

There are several major obstacles to the utilization of social science knowledge. (1) There is frequently no institution or agency to note such knowledge and act upon it. (2) In many instances the social sciences provide accurate descriptions or predictions of events, but no solution to the problem. It is too easy to reject such relevant knowledge out of hand, in the belief that it is simply troublesome when it provides no answers. (3) Some reject social science knowledge because it is threatening to their own views, or to the security of their personal situations during periods of social change. (4) Some reject social science knowledge even when they agree with it, when the resources needed to attain the indicated solutions are too demanding. Even in a nation as wealthy as ours, resources are limited, and policies based on social science findings must compete in the political arena for implementation. Whether or not the nation will use the social sciences in a given instance depends upon the outcome of this political competition.

Although our concern is to increase the use of existing knowledge, the Commission fully recognizes the importance to the nation of public and private support for objective social research to provide a knowledge base from which applied insights and policy formation can proceed. Even the present utilization of the knowledge and insights of the social sciences is possible only because of the preceding half-century of such basic research. Accordingly, we urge that implementation of the Commission's proposals and recommendations in no way deter the growth of the indispensable companion support for basic research in these sciences.

The major recommendations below, then, are designed to increase and improve the nation's utilization of the strengths of the social sciences. The specific plans and suggestions to implement these general recommendations of the Commission are presented in the body of the report.

The Social Sciences and the Professions

The professions are among the main institutions through which social science knowledge can be translated into day-to-day practice. During the past several decades the contribution of the social sciences to professional practice has been increasing. Education has been most notable in this respect; but medicine and public health, social work, and (more recently) law, have also made effective use of such knowledge.

Still, the expressed demand by the professions for social science contributions is infrequent and generally unsystematic. The Commission reviewed the utilization of the social sciences by seven professions: education, engineering, journalism, law, medicine and public health, mental health, and social work. Those sections of the report dealing with each profession contain many specific recommendations for action in accord with the Commission's general conclusions, which are the following:

• *Professional schools should include in their curricula more of the social science knowledge relevant to the particular profession.* With professional schools supplying the leadership, resources for staffing schools with social scientists should be provided from federal, state, foundation, and university funds. Three fundamentals must be observed in this staffing process. (a) The object is not to make social scientists of the professionals, but to assure their exposure to the methodology, capabilities, and knowledge of the social sciences relevant to that profession; (b) the social scientists must retain association with their particular discipline to insure continued competence in that discipline; and (c) there must be institutional recognition of such collaboration, in the form of salary, promotion, and status.

• *Provision must be made for increasing collaborative social science-professional research efforts—not only on basic scientific questions of common interest, but also in joint attacks on social problems within the compass of the specific profession.* The Commission views the funding of such collaborative studies both as a responsibility of the federal government, and as an opportunity for private organizations. The social problem research institutes, to be described below, should provide a valuable institutional base for this type of attack.

The Social Sciences and the Federal Government

The Social Sciences at the White House and Departmental Level

At those levels in the federal government where major policy is made, the social sciences should be deeply involved. Policies for handling the nation's most pressing issues and problems—whether they relate to the cities, pollution, inflation, or supersonic transport —must rest not only on knowledge drawn from the physical and biological sciences, but also on the best available knowledge about human individual and social behavior. Many of our most urgent domestic policy issues, indeed, are more closely related to the social sciences than to the other sciences. Social sciences must be treated, not in isolation, but in their proper position as a part of the entire national pool of scientific and technological knowledge and skill.

• *The new policy of appointing social scientists to membership on the President's Science Advisory Committee should be continued, and the social science members increased, to assure identification of the social science knowledge that should be available to the Committee.*

• *Professional social scientists with backgrounds in relevant areas should be added to, and become an important part of, the Office of Science and Technology staff.* While able staff members drawn from the other sciences have given vigorous and intelligent assistance to panels dealing with such topics as the development of the social sciences, and educational research and development, there have as yet been no appointments of social scientists to the OST.

The Commission recognizes the current interest in establishing a Council of Social Advisers in the White House Office, to serve an advisory role parallel to that of the Council of Economic Advisers. While we strongly agree that social science data should be fully and effectively transmitted to the Administration, we are not prepared to recommend the establishment of such a Council. The Commission has become convinced that this goal can be achieved more efficiently by the inclusion of appropriate social scientists in such key advisory groups as PSAC and OST, and through action by the Council of Economic Advisers.

• *We urge the CEA to give explicit attention to the need for including in its professional staff and consultants: (1) persons drawn from the relevant social sciences outside economics, and (2) persons drawn from the physical sciences and engineering who can bring to bear relevant knowledge about scientific and technological trends and developments.*

Effective Employment of Social Sciences in Government Agencies

Social scientists properly belong at all staff levels and in all functions in federal agencies where they can contribute importantly to performance of their agencies' mission.

• *The Commission recommends strengthening and extension of present practices of employment of social scientists in the federal government, and specifically recommends that an extensive program of periodic leaves of one academic term at full salary (comparable to academic sabbatical leaves) be instituted to enable professional employees to bring themselves up-to-date with the very rapid developments of their own and related disciplines—either by means of specially-designed refresher courses, or by working on research of their own choosing.* Even research not directly related to their employment can contribute effectively to the currency of their knowledge. Eligibility for such leave should be based upon continuous employment with the federal government as a whole rather than with any individual agency.

Because the federal government employs a great number of professional people throughout the country—only 10 per cent of all employees are based in Washington—it should consider multiple programs through which updating can be offered. The federal agencies and the Civil Service Commission as well as the colleges and universities must cooperate in this endeavor. Federal agencies have authority to carry out such programs under the Federal Government Training Act of 1958; and several agencies, such as the National Institutes of Health, have already adopted such a program.

Providing Better Social Science Data

Regularly collected statistical data describing the people in American society and their major institutions have been valuable in the development of successful policy formation and execution. Growing reliance on statistical data for policy decisions has led to an increased demand for data that can be used for projection and prediction. Over the years the social sciences have developed an ever greater capacity for measuring, evaluating, and predicting social change; at the same time the federal government has developed an increasing commitment to serve as a positive force in bringing about such change.

Although there are still large areas of uncertainty in the social sciences, although there are limits to the programs government can effectively manage, and although there are constitutional and political limits to the extension of federal authority, these two trends have converged to produce a strong interest in the further development of statistical time-series data (i.e., social statistics).

• *To improve the quality, range, and utilization of social statistics, the federal government should provide for increased linkages between the bodies of data now routinely collected.* This must, of course, go hand in hand with both federal and private efforts to develop the means for protection of privacy. (Such data linkages and access to data centers should not be allowed, indeed, unless individual and institutional privacy can be protected.)

• *The federal government, universities, and private funding groups should provide the resources necessary for both government and private research organizations to develop new, more frequent, and better social statistics to record the important aspects of American life as yet relatively unstudied.*

The Social Sciences and Business and Labor

Business leaders and social scientists have increasingly found areas where they have mutual interests. Executives have been alerted to the complexities of knowledge required for effective decision-making, and social scientists have found that large business organizations provide living laboratories for observation and analysis. Business schools now provide technical training in economics, and in principles of organization and decision-making processes that employ mathematical and statistical techniques. They are also making efforts to expand their social science staffs. Corporations have recruited social research in such sensitive areas as the introduction and management of change, and have extended these lessons to programs recently developed for recruiting and training hardcore unemployed.

Organized labor and collective bargaining present additional opportunities for the application of the social sciences. Statistical information has been used to relate economic and social characteristics of the collective bargaining environment to the multifaceted decisions that must be made. Labor unions have turned to the social sciences for assistance in adapting their structures and activities to rapidly changing structures in corporation, markets, the economy, and society generally. Social scientists have found living laboratories in labor union organizations that are as vital and dynamic as the business enterprise.

Business firms and labor unions have turned to the social sciences whenever they have seen prospects of gains to the organization. Recognition of the advantages of interchanges between the social sciences on one hand, and business and labor on the other, has been instrumental in establishing important relationships. The past, however, has reaped only a small portion of the potential benefits.

• *The Commission urges the officials in business and labor organizations to strengthen and broaden their existing associations with the social sciences.*

The Social Sciences and Community Organizations

It is the Commission's view that efforts should be made to appraise the opportunities for direct social science application to the work of community organizations. A primary need is a comprehensive inventory, on a national basis, of the social science work going on in community organizations. This should identify the notable successes, in order to isolate the common elements in such successful collaboration. Identification of successful programs, however, is not possible until better evaluative research studies are carried out on community-organization programs.

• *Accordingly, careful evaluation studies of the effectiveness of community organizations should be greatly expanded.*

A systematic appraisal is required of the opportunities for social science to be brought to bear in community organizations. Without such an appraisal, there can be no basis for sound planning to develop further collaboration between the social sciences and community organizations.

• *Accordingly, such an appraisal should be undertaken—either by appropriate federal agencies, or through a task force or commission sponsored from the private sector.*

Since successful demonstrations of social science contributions already exist in some number, the Commission wishes, at the same time, to encourage the support of existing channels for the dissemination of such knowledge. Most typically, the transfer of useful information takes place through social scientists in various relationships to community organizations—consulting, for example— and through the employment of social scientists in a staff or research capacity for a short- or long-term period. Information is also transferred through workshops, institutes, and conferences between organization representatives and social scientists.

After these recommendations concerning social scientists and community organizations have been implemented, it is desirable that there should be available to such organizations—perhaps through an appropriate government organization—opportunity to gain an assessment of how they might benefit from social science knowledge and techniques. Funds should then be made available to the community organizations themselves in order to implement well-planned requests. We believe that community organizations, both public and private, are definite frontiers of possible social science utilization and, as such, deserve systematic exploration.

The Social Sciences and the Public

Improved dissemination of social science knowledge to the public is desirable. (1) The knowledge and insights of the social sciences are directly applicable by each individual to his own life—particularly in such areas as career planning, childrearing, and voluntary community activities. (2) A more receptive attitude and increased knowledge among the general public will raise the public expectations as to the value of social science in dealing with public problems.

To improve the direct utilization of social science knowledge by the public through elementary and secondary school education, and continuing education for adults, the following are recommended:

• *The National Science Foundation should increase its support of efforts to improve social science curricula, and it should encourage the professional social science associations to take responsibility for developing curriculum materials.*

• *Social science associations and funding organizations should encourage the efforts of scholars studying how children develop over time an understanding of basic social science concepts; special attention should be given to the implications of this research for redesigning the elementary and secondary school social science curriculum.*

To improve the direct utilization of social science knowledge by the public through continuing education for adults, the following is recommended:

• *Consideration should be given to launching new federal efforts to develop and increase the social science component of continuing education programs. More funds should be assigned to the appropriate divisions of the Office of Education so that it can add professional and technical staff for this purpose, and additional effort should be made through other appropriate agencies, perhaps the National Science Foundation or the National Endowment for the Humanities. Grants to continuing education organizations, primarily university-based but not solely so, should be made to enable these organizations to further develop their work in the social sciences.*

The mass media provide an effective means of educating the public about the social sciences. Television programing presents a large and unrealized opportunity for social science education, and the Commission believes that much more can be done in the other media also—through magazine articles, newspaper reporting, and books. A number of specific recommendations have been developed by the Commission to increase and improve the mass media reporting of social science knowledge, and these are stated in detail in the body of the report.

Social Problem Research Institutes

Engaging the best of our social science resources to meet contemporary social problems requires the establishment of a new kind of institute with the clearly defined purpose of conducting applied social science research on problems of public significance. The Commission proposes the formation of special social problem research institutes where social problems will be analyzed by teams of specialists from the social sciences and other sciences and professions. Engineers and other professionals must join with social scientists in these efforts. Their technical knowledge is indispensable to any analysis of causes of and solutions to various social problems. Furthermore, each institute must establish close relationships with the agencies or organizations faced with the problem and responsible for its solution at the policy and action level, so that the implication of the institute's studies can be carried forward to the development of policy alternatives and action programs.

In proposing the formation of social problem research institutes, the Commission seeks to bring change to the management of applied social science. The present organization of social science research is not well oriented to attacks on national social issues. The Commission believes that the proposed institutes offer a reasonable hope for more rapid progress in the utilization of social science knowledge. New social problem research institutes will provide a means for implementing many of the recommendations made previously in the report, namely, increased collaboration between the social sciences and the professions, provision of social science knowledge to community organizations, liaisons with business and labor, and more effective transmission of social science information to government.

There have been a number of important attempts to develop this type of institute, and these have had an important influence on social science research and have led the way for the social problem research institutes recommended by the Commission. One can mention specifically the problem-oriented centers established by the Department of Health, Education, and Welfare, and by the Office of Education; and certain nongovernment centers focusing on violence and on manpower problems. Nevertheless, mobilization of social science for solutions to social problems customarily has been ineffective because the problems themselves do not fall solely within the traditional areas of a given social science. Instead, they require for their solution the collaborative focused efforts of the several social sciences, the professions, and other resource groups. Research conducted separately by members of one or another social science rarely provides the necessary broad insights into the nature and resolution of a major social problem. With a few notable exceptions, social research institutes have not been able to broaden their research programs to perform the duties the Commission assigns to the proposed social problem research institutes. The objectives of existing research centers frequently are the development of basic research in a discipline; that is, they are guided by the theoretical interests of the developing science rather than by the need for a solution of current social problems. Even those research centers with an applied social problem orientation usually emphasize a single scientific discipline; or, their research clientele is business and the subject matter fundamentally related to a specific firm's concerns; or, when governmental, they tend to be either short-range in outlook or focused closely upon a specific agency's mission. Such research is valuable to its clients, and there is undoubtedly a genuine need to increase it, but it does not possess the interdisciplinary scope needed for the study of complex social problems. The proposed social problem research institutes will provide an essential missing element in the process of bringing social science research to fuller utilization at the policy-making and action level.

The Commission believes that several problem research institutes are needed so that each then can deal with a specific social problem and be organized more effectively than would be the case if a single institute were spread thinly over a wide variety of social concerns. Moreover, such pluralism gives the opportunity for having several institutes whose subject matters and research projects overlap and thus provide the benefits of diversity and competition that are not likely to emerge from a very large but single national institute. And, a larger number of sharply focused institutes means they can be established throughout the country at universities and in urban centers, which will add to the diversity of analyses, perspectives, and insights.

The Commission therefore recommends the following:
• *$10 million should be appropriated in fiscal year 1970 to the National Science Foundation for the establishment of social problem research institutes; this budget should incease in subsequent years as the institutes mature and to allow for increasing numbers with an objective of about twenty-five institutes.*

Firm commitments should be made to underwrite the full costs of the social problem research institutes during the first years of each institute's life; commitments for funds should be reduced to 20 or 25 per cent of probable expenses as soon as the institutes can compete for research support.

In establishing these institutes by competition among interested universities and other organizations, the following criteria should be operative:
(1) a capable interdisciplinary professional staff that will concentrate its efforts on the chosen subject;

(2) the identification of appropriate client-sponsors, either within or without the federal government, and a proposed way to communicate with and respond to the client-sponsor;

(3) the establishment of appropriate mechanisms to insure a flow of qualified and experienced people through the institute into the user agencies.

If it is apparent from the quality of the proposals for attack on a given social problem that effective resources cannot yet be mobilized in an institute form, the National Science Foundation should not feel constrained to establish an untimely institute. It should, however, explore each such field to learn the difficulties and obstacles, in the expectation that these may be removed.

CONTENTS

I

THE PURPOSE OF
THE SPECIAL
COMMISSION

The Charge to the Commission

In establishing the Special Commission on the Social Sciences in 1968, the National Science Board requested that it prepare analyses and recommendations to improve the application of social science knowledge to significant social problems. The request was stated in the following terms:

> The Special Commission on the Social Sciences has been asked to address itself to the following:
> 1. A statement and analysis of the mechanisms and institutions, societal and governmental, that are needed so that the understanding and knowledge gained by the social sciences may be drawn upon and used effectively when they are relevant to understanding and dealing with significant problems in our society.
> 2. An analysis of what forms of collaboration may be necessary among the social and natural sciences, and engineering, and among their practitioners in addressing these problems; and recommendations concerning how such collaboration might be brought about.
> 3. A statement of what measures and programs, to be administered by federal agencies including the National Science Foundation, are required so that the social sciences may be more effective both in generating new knowledge and in its utilization, and so that our society can gain maximum benefit from the growing knowledge derived from fundamental research in social sciences.

How the Commission sought to meet this charge, and the historical context in which it viewed its work, are set forth in this introductory section.

New Interest in the Uses of Social Science

There has been a long history of effective, if now and then stormy, relationships between the social sciences and other institutions

1

(both governmental and nongovernmental) in American society. For the federal government, in particular, a forthcoming volume[1] describes this history for the past six decades. Among its many instances are: the use of economics in national-income reporting and in implementing the Employment Act of 1946; the use of sample survey techniques in the Department of Agriculture in the late 1930's; the role of opinion research in facilitating the design of acceptable labor-mobilization and food-rationing systems during World War II; the use of psychological testing by the armed services in World Wars I and II and in the selection of Peace Corps and Civil Service workers; the challenge to (and influence on) the policies of the Narcotics Bureau regarding drug use and its treatment by the research findings of psychologists and sociologists; the use by the Office of Statistical Standards of the Bureau of the Budget of social science advisory committees.

The uses of social science outside the federal government since the turn of the century are extensively documented in many scholarly studies.[2] The use of survey research techniques in business, labor, and education; the contributions to business and industrial management of economics, industrial psychology, and sociology; the continuing contribution to methods of teaching from basic research on learning and child development in psychology—all these are good illustrative cases.

Opinion in federal, state, and local governments and in the nation generally about social science has changed in a favorable direction in the past half-dozen years or so. Social scientists are in increasing demand as consultants to public and private organizations. More and more of them are asked to leave their university positions and take employment in government, corporations, community service organizations, hospitals, schools, and many other settings. Economics, psychology, sociology, political science, and their sister social sciences are getting increasing attention in the mass media and in public discussion. Undergraduate and graduate enrollments continue to rise rapidly.

At the federal level, this interest was clearly reflected in the Reuss Committee staff inquiry in 1967 on the nature and value of the social sciences. Committee hearings highlighted a need for more basic research, applied research, and mission-oriented research for government programs, and improved communication with administrators of large-scale programs for dissemination of research findings. Other expressions of concern to increase social

---

[1] Gene M. Lyons, *The Uneasy Partnership: Social Science and the Federal Government in the Twentieth Century* (New York: Russell Sage Foundation, 1969).
[2] E.g., P. F. Lazarsfeld *et al.*, *The Uses of Sociology* (New York: Basic Books, Inc., 1967).

science utilization are the proposed legislation for the establishment of a National Social Science Foundation, the proposed legislation for a "Full Opportunity and Social Accounting Act," and the recently passed Daddario-Kennedy legislation changing the charter and adding the social sciences to the responsibilities of the National Science Foundation.[3]

Recent and current national commissions and study groups also attest to the new growth of interest: The Advisory Committee on Government Programs in the Behavioral Sciences of the National Academy of Science–National Research Council published its report in the fall of 1968.[4] The Behavioral and Social Science Survey sponsored by the National Academy of Science–National Research Council and the Social Science Research Council—a study devoted to appraising the current and future needs of the social sciences— will submit its report in the summer of 1969.[5]

This heightened interest, while most welcome, is still inadequate and much more can be done to further social science utilization. Too small a fraction of the national research effort is being devoted to social science; and it is the opinion of this Commission that the nation is missing crucial opportunities to utilize the best of social science in the formation and evaluation of policies for achieving desired social goals.

Unrealized Opportunities for Utilization

The Commission believes that among the American people there are a number of widely shared national and community objectives, and that social scientists can contribute to their achievement. Interethnic and interracial conflict; alienation of much of America's youth from society; multiple problems of man living in urban settings; various pollutions of man's environment; crime; mental illness rates; problems of alcoholic and narcotic addiction; problems of the educational process in the nation's schools—these are among the most visible and publicized concerns.

---

[3] See *The Use of Social Research in Federal Domestic Programs,* a staff study for the Research and Technical Programs Subcommittee of the Committee on Government Operations, House of Representatives, Representative Henry S. Reuss, Chairman (Washington, D.C.: Government Printing Office, 1967); and *National Foundation for the Social Sciences,* Hearings before the Subcommittee on Government Research of the Committee on Government Operations, Senate, Senator Fred R. Harris, Chairman (Washington, D.C.: Government Printing Office, 1967). See also the bibliography "Some Recent Congressional and Other Publications Relating to NSF or the Social Sciences," *P.S.* (Newsletter of the American Political Science Association), I (Spring, 1968), 45–46. In 1968 Congress also included in the mandate of the National Endowment for the Humanities such fields as history and linguistics.

[4] Advisory Committee on Government Programs in the Behavioral Sciences, *The Behavioral Sciences and the Federal Government* (Washington, D.C.: National Research Council–National Academy of Sciences, 1968).

[5] For a description of similar efforts since the end of World War II, see Lyons, *op. cit.,* Chap. 8.

The Commission strongly believes that the research methods and concepts of the social sciences are valuable assets in attacking these problems, and in the achievement of national and local goals. For instance, social science can contribute importantly toward solving the problem of the successful delivery of health services— in accordance with the best medical and public health knowledge —to the entire urban population. Understanding of the sources of effective motivation toward the use of current medical services; successful economic management of medical services; the identification and location of changing population groups now deprived of health services—these are among the many specific questions to which social science can contribute answers.

At present, the social sciences, like the humanities, are a relatively unused national resource. Much of America's effort to achieve its aims makes little attempt to use this fundamental resource. The Commission asserts its doubt that this country can successfully solve its challenging and diverse social problems unless it draws upon the increasing capabilities of the social science community.

Nature of Commission Recommendations

The primary task of this Commission is to make policy recommendations. Its report is directed to improving the national use of the social sciences by such policy recommendations; it is focused on revitalization of existing organizations and the development of new social institutions, in the search for better ways to channel the flow of social science resources into current affairs. The recommendations of the Commission are major proposals that, in our judgment, should have the highest priority because of (a) the enduring consequences that can be expected to follow from their implementation, and (b) the practical feasibility of executing them in the foreseeable future.

Certain recommendations require essentially no increase in expenditures at the community, state, or national level; these improve existing institutions so as to make more effective use of the current resources of the social sciences. Thus, changes in the curriculum of American law schools, changes in staffing policies of selected federal agencies, or shifts in the content of certain mass media programing, can be accomplished with little or no increase in cost. On the other hand, the Commission's recommendations for the establishment of innovative, sometimes costly, organizations will require substantial funds, as, for example, new social problem research institutes, the staffing of community service organizations with social scientists, mid-career fellowships at universities for government employees, the establishment of a social-indicators program, and other proposals set forth in this report.

Basic Research

Although our concern is to increase the use of existing knowledge, the Commission fully recognizes the importance to the nation of public and private support for objective research that provides a knowledge base from which applied insights and policy formation can proceed. Even the current utilization of the knowledge and insights of the social sciences is feasible only because of the preceding half-century of basic research. Accordingly, we urge that implementation of the Commission's proposals and recommendations in no way interfere with the growth of the indispensable companion support of basic research in these sciences.[6]

Organization of the Report

The substance of the Commission report falls into seven main parts. Chapter II presents examples of the uses of the social sciences and an analysis of various obstacles to their greater use. Chapter III deals with Commission recommendations regarding the social sciences in relation to a selected number of the major professions in this country. In Chapter IV, the Commission considers the relationship between social sciences and the federal government. It deals with the use of social science at the White House and Cabinet level, with the staffing of government agencies, and with providing better statistical data to the government. In Chapters V and VI, respectively, the Commission considers the use of the social sciences in business and labor, and in various community organizations. Then in Chapter VII we examine the contributions of social science through the media of public education —both at the elementary and secondary school levels, and at the adult level. Chapter VIII is concerned with increasing the growth of problem-oriented research, and deals with the organization and operation of social problem research institutes.

This report focuses on those groups and organizations which can draw upon social sciences in their operations, rather than concentrating directly on current social problems. Throughout the report, for example, in the sections dealing with the professions, public education, the development of applied research centers, there are

---

[6] The reader is referred to the forthcoming report of the Behavioral and Social Survey Committee, co-sponsored by the National Academy of Sciences–National Research Council and the Social Science Research Council, to obtain detailed information on the basic research needs of the social sciences for manpower, money, and facilities.

recurrent references to the achievement of goals. Race differences; urban problems; educational institutions; concerns about youth; the provision of health services—these and many other national problems are woven into the discussion of institutional mechanisms or professional groups as challenging, substantive themes. Such themes are illustrative but do not pretend to be exhaustive.

Audience and Implementation

The Commission has sought to place certain policy proposals before the group or groups that in its judgment should effect the proposed changes. Some of the specific recommendations might be acted upon and implemented by the National Science Board, either through the programs of the National Science Foundation or through policy positions taken by the National Science Board within the federal government. Other recommendations involve other agencies of government—federal, state, and local. And several proposals can be acted upon effectively only by nongovernmental institutions, among them the major professional associations, private voluntary agencies, private foundations, American corporations, labor unions, and learned societies.

II

THE NATURE AND
USE OF THE
SOCIAL SCIENCES

What Are the Social Sciences?

The social sciences are intellectual disciplines that study man as a social being by means of the scientific method. It is their focus on man as a member of society, and on the groups and societies that he forms, that distinguishes the social sciences from the physical and biological sciences.

Historically, five social sciences have been regarded as central: anthropology, economics, political science, psychology, and sociology. Other important fields that deal with social phenomena are: demography, history, human geography, linguistics, and social statistics.[1]

Anthropology and sociology are somewhat difficult to distinguish from each other. Both study the societies in which man lives, that is, the social forms and structures within which individual and group behavior takes place. *Anthropology* (which includes social anthropology, archaeology, physical anthropology, and the linguistics of preliterate cultures) studies the varied physical and cultural characteristics of man throughout the world. Traditionally, its attention has been directed to primitive cultures. But a number of anthropologists now study the cultures of industrialized societies, including of course the United States; and anthropologists have produced fruitful work on such important contemporary problems as poverty, ghetto life, minority groups, and mental health.

---

[1] Branches of psychology and anthropology often fall in the biological sciences as well as the social sciences. Similarly, parts of historical inquiry properly belong in the humanities. We refer the reader to the forthcoming report of the Behavioral and Social Survey Committee for an exposition of the nature of these disciplines, their development, and the kind of work that each does. We also leave to that report the tasks (1) of describing the hybrid fields that exist within the social sciences, and between the social sciences and the natural sciences; and (2) of distinguishing between behavioral sciences and social sciences.

Sociology is often called the science of society. In contrast to anthropology, sociology has always concentrated on the structure and functioning of groups within literate societies. Sociologists study such features of society as the family, rural and urban life, race relations, crime, and occupational groupings.[2]

Economics is the study of the allocation of scarce productive resources among competing uses. Within this framework, economists engage in theoretical and empirical research on macroeconomic subjects—reaching and maintaining full employment, avoiding inflation and deflation, understanding and promoting economic growth, analyzing fiscal and monetary policies, defining balance and imbalance in international payments; also on microeconomic subjects—market pricing, monopolies, manpower, labor markets, union movements, farm issues, and problems resulting from inequalities in income distribution and poverty.

Psychology studies the nature and organization of mental processes in man. Psychologists deal with man's mental abilities and aptitudes, his capacities for learning, for thinking, for emotional expression, and for motivation. Psychologists have developed intelligence and aptitude tests for a great variety of uses. They work on problems of learning in education, problems of personnel selection in industry, and problems of clinical assessment in mental illness, among many others.

Political Science investigates the ways in which men govern themselves. It is concerned with the goals of the political system, the structural relationships in that system, the patterns of individual and group behavior which help explain how that system functions, and the policy outputs as well as behavioral consequences of that system. Political scientists study a variety of phenomena involved in the process of government, including political parties, interest groups, public opinion and communication, bureaucracy, international relations, and administration.

These, then, are the five central social science disciplines. We turn now to short descriptions of the fields that are closely related to the social sciences.

Demography is the science of population. It studies the composition and movement of human populations—births, deaths, life expectancy, and migration. Demographers work on large-scale manpower problems to estimate and predict the numbers of persons in given categories of interest—for example, the number of voters in the states to determine how many members each state will

---

[2] *Social psychology* is an important subfield that sociology shares with psychology. Social psychology studies the behavior of man as influenced by the groups to which he belongs.

have in the House of Representatives, and the number of men likely to be available for military service at some future date.

History has two well-known aims: to reconstruct events of the past from records and artifacts made near the time of the events, and to analyze why events occurred as they did. Historians contribute a valuable perspective to analysis of current activities by providing a sense of continuity over time; and their analysis of persons, movements, events, and concepts in the past is extremely helpful in much other social science research.

Human Geography has two intertwined foci: the relationships between man and his natural and manmade environments, and the patterns and processes of spatial organization. It has associated increasingly with other sciences, and shares many social science concerns and methods of inquiry. Geographers study such problems as the spread of new ideas between places; the perception and control of environmental hazards such as floods and drought; and the general spatial organization of metropolitan areas including such items as land value patterns, planning of human and environmental systems, and intraurban migrations.

Linguistics elicits language data to produce insights into the structure of language and the meaning of specific language units. It investigates the basic characteristics of many languages—their sound systems, grammatical categories, and rules of syntax. In this study of particular languages, linguistics seeks to understand language in general. Anthropologists and linguists share an interest in the unwritten language of primitive peoples; and the language of a people tells the anthropologist a great deal about the culture and its origins. The language of an individual speaker reveals information about social status, geographic origin, and personality that are of interest to the psychologist and sociologist. Psycholinguists study how children learn to use language.

The theory of *statistics* has broad applicability in all the sciences; but specific techniques have been developed for the specific research needs of the social sciences. Multiple correlation and regression have been developed to substitute for controlled laboratory experimentation. Sampling procedures; factor analysis; handling of nonnormally distributed observations; testing of hypotheses and estimation of parameters from nonexperimental data; decision theory and nonparametric testing—these are methodological developments particularly important to social science.

The brief descriptions above separate the social sciences on the basis of their substantive concerns. Equally important are their common methods of inquiry. They all live by the "scientific method," that is, they seek publicly verifiable, and hence cumulative, knowledge. Speculation about the nature of social phenomena is never sufficient by itself; empirical tests of speculative propositions are an integral part of these disciplines, as is the estimation of the numerical frequency of cited instances.

Experimentation, central to the scientific method as practiced in the physical and biological sciences, is relatively absent from the social sciences. Only in psychology has a substantial amount of experimentation been carried out. Two reasons for this omission have been the lack until recently of experimental techniques, and the great costs involved in such experiments. There is also the strong moral proscription against experimenting with human beings, which absolutely prohibits some kinds of experiments. Social scientists are often able to approximate experiments, however, and can attain some of the analytic virtues of experimentation through the sophisticated use of statistical controls.

Social scientists try to be as objectively independent as possible of their own biases. Obviously, no scientist in the social area can be completely detached from his environment, but social scientists make their methods public so that others may attempt to repeat their work and, thus, appraise their findings.

Our description of the social sciences characterizes them as academic disciplines. Academic social scientists are primarily interested in pursuing basic research problems within their respective disciplines. They often pay relatively little attention to practical applications of their disciplines, though their interest in this area is increasing. Many do consult on applied problems for organizations outside universities. There are also a number of recognized applied specialties—industrial relations, city planning, economic forecasting, criminology, and educational psychology, among others. But even where these constitute formal fields of study, they tend to be given secondary status in the prestige structure of the university.

Much (and varied) applied work is, however, going on outside the colleges and universities—in government, business, and independent research institutes—which is problem-centered and not discipline-centered. This makes it difficult to classify such research by discipline. A social scientist often works on a problem that has traditionally "belonged" to a discipline other than the one in which he was trained. And one finds non-social scientists (mathematicians, engineers, and computer experts) increasingly working on problems that social scientists have traditionally regarded as their own.

It is clear to the Commission that the social sciences have developed acceptable scientific procedures to collect valid information about the problems they confront. They have substantially increased their body of knowledge over the past decades. They have also developed excellent methods of analysis and evaluation for testing theoretical and practical propositions. And even where great gaps of knowledge remain, the social scientists' experience can offer invaluable intuitive understanding and special insight. The Commission does note, however, that because of these gaps, and because of the complexity of the social world, social scientists are not always prepared to formulate appropriate hypotheses for testing.

Practical Uses of the Social Sciences

The caveat above does not imply that the social sciences cannot help the nation solve its social problems. The Commission is convinced, indeed, that the social sciences *can* contribute significantly to solving the nation's problems if full advantage is taken of their strengths. They have, in fact, already made many contributions. Social scientists manifestly must be consulted in the collection of relevant information and in evaluating social policies already in existence. Their knowledge and informed intelligence should be sought out (along with other sources of advice) before social programs are instituted, so that faults in social program design may be detected and avoided in advance. Social scientists can be particularly valuable in program design by pointing out deficiencies in the conventional wisdom on which planners may be relying.

It may be obvious to say that social scientists ought to be entrusted with tasks they are clearly capable of carrying out. Nevertheless, the Commission wishes to stress that even in areas where all knowledge is still uncertain, consultation with social scientists may well be in order. Their firm commitment to basic research will undoubtedly continue to convert their intuitive understanding into knowledge.

The following two examples illustrate how knowledge, methods of data collection, and methods of evaluation can be combined to solve problems:

1. Basic research in economics provided the knowledge necessary to avoid recurrence of the prolonged economic declines of the 1920's and 1930's. The most important contributions were (a) the development of a system of national-income accounts, and (b) the theory of income determination in terms of both monetary and fiscal variables. The interrelation of the two provided the conceptual

structure and the information system to determine what happens in an economy and to make predictions about the future. Research into the applications of this knowledge provided governments with alternative strategies and policies for economic stabilization, and the result has been exceptional economic stability since 1945.

We should not be complacent, however. The history of economic stabilization since the end of World War II has not been uniformly successful. Governmental forecasts in 1945 of massive unemployment turned out to be simply wrong. In addition, the period since 1945 has been characterized by an inability to achieve both full employment with vigorous growth and at the same time stable prices. These failures are at least partially due to the inadequacy of knowledge in the area of economic stabilization, and more needs to be done.

2. A second example of an important social science contribution has been the creation of psychological tests to select persons with specific abilities. Enough knowledge has accumulated so that many kinds of mental and motor skills may be measured and predicted reasonably well by means of tests based on that research. One of the best of these tests, developed by the Educational Testing Service, is the Scholastic Achievement Test (SAT), which has been in continuous use since 1926. Its purpose is to measure the level of development of the verbal and mathematical skills necessary to perform the academic tasks required in college. At colleges where the SAT has been used as part of the admissions process for the last twenty or thirty years, the academic failures of enrolled students have been materially reduced.

The SAT is important because it is more efficient in matching persons with tasks they have the ability to perform than were previous selection procedures. This advantage applies to all successful psychological tests. Second, the SAT supplies a universal standard for comparing students, which makes it more difficult for social class, ethnicity, race, and religion to be used prejudicially in selection. The Educational Testing Service reports, for example, that

> . . . in the Ivy League colleges . . . the undergraduate body of the 1920's was a homogeneous group with respect to socioeconomic background and a heterogeneous one with respect to intellectual ability. Today the picture is almost reversed—undergraduates in these colleges come from widely varying socioeconomic backgrounds and possess a generally high intellectual ability.[3]

There has been a good deal of criticism of the SAT and similar tests, however. Some students with high SAT scores do not do sat-

---

[3] Educational Testing Service, *Annual Report 1961–1962*, 45–46.

isfactory college work, and others with low SAT scores do well in college. The test is not able to take into account environmental effects, the motivational level of the student, or other factors on which college grades are assigned. Moreover, there are obviously other intellectual abilities besides the verbal and mathematical abilities on which the test is based. To ignore them in a nationwide selection instrument such as the SAT may mean that potentials are ignored that, if developed, would benefit both the persons who possess them and the nation as a whole. Clearly, further research is necessary here also.

Although the variety of uses of the social sciences has been considerable, their success has varied.[4] The following accounts of applied work in demography, political science, and sociology give some idea of that variety.

Demography. The information produced by demographers in the study of population growth and of the migration of people in the United States has provided the basis for long-range planning by many of the most important sectors and institutions in American society. The United States Bureau of the Census has played the leading role in this work. Population projections, combined with migration data, provide the basis for long-range planning by the telephone companies and other public utilities. Population projections, such as given in volumes based on the 1950 Census (e.g., *America's Children*), also provide the basis for effective programing on the part of school boards, school suppliers, highway commissions, toy manufacturers, and the children's garment industry, to name just a few.[5] Moreover, the studies of population movement and distribution in urban areas have provided the basis for planning of the timing and placement of branches of department stores, savings banks, commercial banks, gasoline stations, and other major American enterprises. One must conclude that the effective deployment of investment and manpower in these many different aspects of American life was substantially improved by the use of demographic information.

Political science. Political scientists have continuously engaged in assessing various aspects of the political system, often leading to significant proposals for reform. Proposals in the field of "public administration"—leading to the Civil Service system, centralized budgeting, and the city-manager concept—are illustrative. Simi-

---

[4] The reader is referred to the forthcoming book by Gene Lyons, *op. cit.*, for a history of the use of social science by the federal government.
[5] Eleanor H. Bernert, *America's Children* (New York: John Wiley & Sons, Inc., 1958).

larly, Congressional and state legislative reform (e.g., the Legislative Reorganization Act of 1946) can be traced in part to the critical evaluations of political scientists, as can such reforms as the direct primary; the short ballot; the regulation of party finance; the regulation of lobbying; improvements in election administration; and more responsible and disciplined party organization.

In recent years the Supreme Court's decisions on legislative reapportionment (*Baker* v. *Carry,* 1962, and subsequent decisions of 1964) were preceded and followed by specific political science studies of the theoretical and technical questions of malapportionment and reapportionment. Today, as previously, political science is involved in study, observation, and evaluation of the political system and its subsystems of action—whether of the operation of the city and county government in their own local environments; or the functioning of state and national legislative, executive, administrative, and judicial agencies of government.

Sociology. Sociologists have worked on practical problems in a large number of different fields including law, medicine, social work, business, criminology, education, public health, and gerontology. Their major research tool is the sample survey, which has been skillfully used to collect information on a vast number of questions pertinent to these different fields. The whole field of market research would not be possible without the sample survey; no other technique collects reliable information on consumer behavior as quickly and as cheaply. Sociologists (as well as psychologists) have also been centrally involved in the development of political polling, a field that is becoming increasingly sophisticated and increasingly important to persons who are directly involved in politics.

Sociologists have worked on a number of important substantive problems, of which the following are two examples:

1. Sociologists have contributed to the new understanding of the magnitude of crime in the nation through the measurement of rates of criminal acts based on reports by victims of crimes. Their studies show that estimates based on arrests for criminal acts grossly understate the estimates based on reports by victims.

2. Sociologists have shown that for the same level of talent, fewer persons of low socioeconomic status receive advanced educational training than persons of high socioeconomic status. This talent loss has concerned many persons since the end of World War II and has led to remedial measures, such as the expansion of state universities, the establishment of new scholarship and loan

resources, and the creation of federal programs like Upward Bound, Talent Search, and VISTA. Research by sociologists in this area has helped to bring about the present national concern and to describe the situation in such a way that effective action can be taken.

Obstacles to the Use of the Social Sciences

Well-recognized obstacles to the utilization of social science knowledge lie within the social sciences themselves, and social scientists must share the blame for the failure to apply social science more broadly. Most professional social scientists are employed in academic institutions where their nonteaching activities are focused on their academic institution and their research. The research emphasis is on the building up of the basic theoretical structure of the disciplines. And the social scientist who works on applied problems is often viewed as a second-class citizen—regarded by his academic peers as inferior to colleagues who do basic research.

Empirical research tends to be exploratory, or for the purpose of testing theoretical propositions, rather than for practical problem-solving. Even when social science work is directed to application, it often produces fragments of knowledge that need to be joined with other fragments to present a program of action. Until this is accomplished these fragments lie around, as John W. Gardner has put it, like loose bricks in a brickyard.

Furthermore, when social scientists have been called upon as consultants in practical situations, many have failed to deliver. Two general complaints have been voiced about social scientists as consultants. First, communication has been impeded because social scientists speak in a jargon incomprehensible to the layman. Social scientists are ordinarily able to translate their own technical language into terms more understandable to a layman, and should make more of an effort to do so. But the problem is partly due to the layman. He is often unwilling to make any effort to learn concepts—and the technical language—of those he consults.

Social scientists fail to meet demands on them in a second way. When faced with a specific problem that has no ready-made conceptual answer, they frequently retreat to the laboratory for more research and more facts. But the client would ordinarily settle for less than a scientifically adequate answer. He simply wants the consultant to apply his trained intelligence, and give help based on the information on hand. When the consultant tells him he has formulated his problem in such a way that advice is impossible, too often the client retreats to his office. And often any reformulation the consultant suggests is ignored, to the detriment of communication between them.

These are familiar problems of long standing. In addition to them, the Commission identifies five other major obstacles. No one of these obstacles is unique to the social sciences, and each of them is only a partial obstacle.

1. Lack of clients.
2. The distinct roles of social scientist and policy-maker.
3. Implications that threaten the status quo.
4. Financial limitations.
5. Political process.

Lack of clients. There is frequently no institution or agency to take up new knowledge and act upon it. In such instances the facts produced by the social sciences find no felt need among the people to whom they are relevant. Perhaps the knowledge is not perceived as significant, or perhaps there are no effective mechanisms to translate the public need into action.

A good example is provided by the work of Robin M. Williams, Jr., Professor of Sociology at Cornell University. In 1947, Williams predicted that the nation would face race riots and other violence as Negro aspirations in the United States were raised. He stated this view in the following terms:

> Mass violence (e.g., race riots) is most likely under the following conditions: (a) prolonged frustration, leading to a high tension level; (b) presence of population elements with a propensity to violence (especially lower class, adolescent males in socially disorganized areas); (c) a highly visible and rapid change in intergroup relations; (d) a precipitating incident of intergroup conflict.
>
> Militancy, except for sporadic and short-lived uprisings, is not characteristic of the most deprived and oppressed groups, but rather of those who have gained considerable rights so that they are able realistically to hope for more.
>
> A militant reaction from a minority group is most likely when (a) the group's position is rapidly improving, or (b) when it is rapidly deteriorating, especially if this follows a period of improvement.[5]

This prediction went unheard. The prevailing view was that a continuing assault on the problems of prejudice and segregation would lead to peaceful solution of this historic problem. Little attention was given to the possibility of increasing militancy among Negroes as integration proceeded. The events of the 1960's proved

---

[5] Robin M. Williams, Jr., *The Reduction of Intergroup Tensions* (New York: Social Science Research Council, 1947), 60–61.

Williams correct. But only after the fact did this social science knowledge come to the center of the stage and be viewed as significant for national, state, and local policy formation.

It would be easy for the skeptic to say that we are using hindsight here. No one was listening to a lot of other suggestions by social scientists that turned out to be incorrect. But this prediction by Williams did have a great deal of support; it was based on much empirical evidence; it was shared by a number of other respected sociologists in the field of race relations; and it was generally accepted by the field of sociology.

The distinct roles of social scientist and policy-maker. A second obstacle occurs because the role of social scientist is distinct from the role of policy-maker. Traditionally, it has been the responsibility of the social scientist to provide accurate description or prediction about a given problem, not to provide a practical solution to it. But it is easy for a policy-maker to reject social science knowledge simply because it is not presented in the form of a practical solution.

The Coleman Report is a good example.[6] The Civil Rights Act of 1964 directed the Commissioner of Education to survey inequalities in educational opportunities for major racial, ethnic, and religious groups in the United States. Several studies were initiated by the National Center for Educational Statistics of the United States Office of Education in accordance with this directive. James S. Coleman, Professor of Sociology at Johns Hopkins University, was asked to direct a national survey of public elementary and secondary schools. Nearly 600,000 students in grades 1, 3, 6, 9, and 12 were interviewed and tested, in about 4,000 schools generally representative of public schools in the United States.

One problem addressed was the extent to which differences in children's achievement test scores are attributable to the influence of the family or of the school. The central finding was the following:

> . . . schools bring little influence to bear on a child's achievement that is independent of his background and general social context; and . . . this very lack of an independent effect means that the inequalities imposed on children by their home, neighborhood, and peer environment are carried along to become the inequalities with which they confront adult life at the end of school. For equality of educational opportunity through the schools must imply a strong effect of schools that is independent of the child's immediate social environment, and that strong independent effect is not present in American schools.[7]

---

[6] James S. Coleman *et al., Equality of Educational Opportunity* (Washington, D.C.: Government Printing Office, 1966).
[7] *Ibid.,* 325.

The common assumption that education can repair any non-biological deficiency in scholastic aptitude that students may have when they begin school is thus clearly called into question. The Coleman Report shows that, on the average, Negroes come into school behind whites, and leave school even farther behind whites, in terms of educational achievement. The social implications of this finding are enormous. But the Coleman Report does not propose measures to remedy this problem since that was not its purpose; it merely reports a disheartening set of facts. The report has received little attention from government at any level, largely because it does not provide a practical solution to the problem that it documents.[8]

Implications that threaten the status quo. Another obstacle to the use of social science knowledge is that people may reject the information because it threatens their own views. For example: Between 1880 and 1901, the United States Government published a 128-volume *War of the Rebellion: A Compilation of Official Records of the Union and Confederate Armies.* The volumes describe the American Negro as a dependable and effective soldier; the same conclusion was reached in three histories dealing with Negro soldiers in the Civil War, all published in the quarter-century after the war.

Yet, as late as 1936, a report of field grade officers at the Army War College on "The Use of Negro Manpower in War" stated:

> . . . the Negro is docile, tractable, light-hearted, care-free, and good-natured. If unjustly treated he is likely to become surly and stubborn though this is a temporary phase. He is careless, shiftless, irresponsible, and secretive. He resents censure and is best handled with praise and ridicule. He is unmoral, untruthful, and his sense of right doing is relatively inferior.[9]

It is doubtful that, if presented with the information from the Civil War, the authors would have changed their views in the least. Perhaps because of this attitude among Army officers the War Department reaffirmed a segregation policy in 1940, despite a nondiscrimination clause in the Selective Service Act of that year.

Or social scientists may point out a problem that people admit but do not want to spend the energy to solve. It is a natural reaction to put out of mind unpleasant facts of life that threaten one

---

[8] It has been pointed out to us that the Coleman Report is too recent (June, 1966) for action to occur. We disagree. It is almost three years since the report was published, time enough for serious remedial action to have at least begun.
[9] Report of Committee 3, Course G–1, "The Use of Negro Manpower in War" (Washington, D.C.: Army War College, November 12, 1936).

and demand sacrifice. Air and water pollution; crowding; various addictions; suicide; emotional disturbances; violence and other aggressive acts—each demanding something of the citizen by way of action and changes in his style of life—all can be viewed as someone else's problem. The question is: How can the knowledge and forecasts of the social sciences be made to *command* the attention of an effective body of citizens to make them face the facts and act before disaster strikes?

Financial limitations. A fourth obstacle is an economic one. Even in a nation as wealthy as ours there is a limit to available resources; and national, local, and personal interests compete for scarce funds. Thus, much social science knowledge with its implications for needed changes competes with other demands on the nation's assets—space exploration; war; faster travel; conservation; oceanographic research; and so on across the range of interests of a large and heterogeneous society.

In the marketplace of competing interests new public programs will obviously meet least resistance when they are to be financed from normal increases in government receipts materializing without changes in tax rates and not endangering current levels of support for other programs. Public programs that require higher rates in existing taxes and cut into the resources of existing programs will be resisted. The extent of opposition can be expected to be most strenuous when a specific group of taxpayers believes its taxes will be earmarked for the benefit of others.

Political process. Finally, the implications of social science findings must complete in the political arena for implementation. The Coleman Report became an object of political controversy, as did the recent Kerner Commission report on riots.[10] Social change— whether arising from social science knowledge or from some other source—threatens to erode the political power of one or another individual or group not interested in sharing or giving up the political position already held. Whether or not the nation will use the social sciences in a given instance depends upon the outcome of the political competition among different vested interests, with all their degrees of approval and disapproval toward any matter at issue.

The aim of the social sciences (in common with all sciences) is

[10] *Report of the National Advisory Commission on Civil Disorders* (New York: The New York Times Company, 1968).

to seek knowledge and provide understanding, not to determine the nation's values. This is an important point. When social science knowledge contributes to the improvement of social programs that flow from widely shared values, there is little likelihood that political controversy will occur. But when social science knowledge suggests that values should change, or that implicit values should be examined and made explicit, political controversy will almost surely arise.

▌▌▌

THE SOCIAL
SCIENCES AND
THE PROFESSIONS

The professions—law, medicine, engineering, social work, journalism, mental health work, and education—are among the main social institutions through which social science knowledge can be translated into day-to-day practice. As Price[1] points out, the professions have a distinctive role in the translation of knowledge to action. In the case of law, social science knowledge is expressed in social reform (through legislation or through judicial decision), and also through the usual practice of law in the office or in the courts. Social science is brought into use in daily medical practice and in the planning and execution of new ventures in public health and the delivery of health care; in the design and construction of homes and institutional buildings; in the decisions of superintendents of schools and State Boards of Education; in the reporting and interpretation of the meaning of events in the daily news by journalists; and in many other instances of professional practice.

The influential power of the professions in American society makes it critical that the social dimensions of their work not be neglected or subordinated to the technical and mechanical aspects. The social sciences can sensitize these professionals to the social consequences of their professional behavior, and alert them to the impact of their professional roles on the well-being of individuals and groups. More than this, of course, the social sciences provide resources both in knowledge and theory that, when joined with the professional's training and practical experience, help achieve the desired ends of a given profession.

The practicing professions must each make use of knowledge gained by basic research, including research in the social sciences.

---

[1] Don K. Price, *The Scientific Estate* (Cambridge, Mass.: Harvard University Press, 1965).

21

All the professions are somehow concerned with people and consequently require some understanding of human behavior. Donald Young noted:

> Reliance for such understanding thus far has been overwhelmingly on lessons drawn rather casually from professional experience by the practitioners themselves. However, leaders in the practicing professions where an understanding of human behavior is clearly of crucial major importance, as in the health services and social work, are becoming increasingly dissatisfied with this traditional and uncertain approach to the problems of social behavior encountered in their specialties.[2]

This Commission concludes from its review that appropriate exposure of students in the professional schools to social science principles, knowledge, and methodology is essential for the optimal development of these future practitioners. The lawyer who is asked to develop separation papers or divorce proceedings, the physician who needs to tell the mother that her child has diabetes, the social worker who needs to prepare the family for prolonged disability on the part of the breadwinner—they all need to understand personality development, family structure, economic needs. The physician who cannot find an appropriate nursing home for a patient with a disabling chronic illness, the engineer who needs to clarify to his client the costs and benefits of alternative designs —both can benefit from an understanding of economic constraints, community standards, expectations, and the decision-making process. Thus, discussions on a case basis of all the diverse forces that can affect the work of any practitioner are fundamental to the optimal preparation of professional school students. And social scientists are indispensable participants in such discussions.

Relevant social science knowledge, methodology, and insight must be incorporated into the curriculum to amplify and provide an added dimension of reality to the discussion of problems and solutions which face the members of that profession. Social scientists should be appointed to the faculty of professional schools to provide teaching at appropriate times, and to facilitate the involvement of social science experts in the conduct of research activities in those schools.

The continued relationship of such faculty to the department of their basic discipline is also crucial. The interest of the basic department in an effective functional relationship with professional schools for both teaching and research is necessary and justified in itself. Furthermore, it is reasonable to expect that research of

---

[2] Donald R. Young, "Sociology and the Practicing Professions," *American Sociological Review*, 20 (December, 1955), 642.

high quality on the problems faced by a profession can lead to methodological refinements and theoretical modifications relevant to the social science discipline per se. Functional linkages with the social problem institutes discussed in Chapter VIII would strengthen the above activities and relationships.

Accordingly, the Commission's recommendations are threefold: The first general recommendation is that professional schools should take the steps necessary to include in their curricula more of the social science knowledge relevant to the particular profession. With professional schools supplying the leadership, resources for staffing schools with social scientists should be provided from both federal and university funds.

Three fundamental principles must be observed in this staffing process. (1) The object is not to make social scientists of the professionals, but to assure their exposure to the methodology, capabilities, and relevance of the social sciences to that profession; (2) the social scientists must retain association with their particular discipline to insure continued competence in that discipline; and (3) there must be institutional recognition of such collaboration, in the form of salary, promotion, and status.

The second general recommendation is the obverse of the first: that more social scientists be exposed to the needs of the various professions for new kinds of knowledge and new research designs.

Both of these general recommendations lead to the third: Provision must be made for increasing collaborative social science-*cum*-professional-research efforts—not only on basic scientific questions of common interest, but also in joint attacks on social problems within the compass of the specific profession.

The Commission views the funding of such collaborative studies both as a responsibility of the federal government, and as an opportunity for private organizations. The problem-oriented research institutes, described below, should provide a valuable institutional base for this type of attack.

In the sections that follow, seven selected professions are discussed as illustrative cases. The discussion presents a brief overview of past and present relationships between the social sciences and each profession, and documents the need for increased utilization of the social sciences.

Education

The profession of education has traditionally enjoyed a close relationship with the social sciences. Current educational practice has been influenced by psychological theories of learning; the results of experiments in social psychology; and sociological research—especially studies of complex organizations, small groups, and intergroup relations. Research specialists within the field of education have relied heavily on techniques developed in the various social sciences to evaluate the effectiveness of new programs, teaching methods, and equipment. Specific social science inventions, such as standardized tests and programed learning devices, have played an important role in educational practice and policy formation during the last fifty years.

Despite this record of social science involvement in education, important gaps still exist in the utilization of social science knowledge by educators. There are various reasons for this.

The separation between schools of education and traditional academic departments in many universities has led to poor communication, and has often resulted in the relative isolation of those social scientists who have chosen to concentrate their efforts on educational problems. Consequently, few attempts have been made either to explore systematically the implications of research done outside the settings where education is traditionally studied (small group studies, experiments in social psychology, and the like) for educational policy and practice, or to develop and test empirically innovative models of educational systems founded on basic research in learning, motivation, and organization. Moreover, although research utilizing social science techniques has become an increasingly important part of the normal operation of school systems and the activities of teacher-training institutions, the great bulk of this research has not been of high enough quality to help solve the exceptionally complicated problems besetting education. Finally, many professionals in education feel that social science has little practical to offer them outside a few specialized areas (such as psychometrics). By the same token, very few social scientists have made any effort to convince educators of the applicability of their findings.

Two key points are implicit in the preceding argument. First, there must be better communication between social scientists and professional educators. Second, social science theory and research may offer significant insights into educational problems that have not yet been explored in a systematic manner. In light of the foregoing considerations, the Commission makes the following recommendations:

First, increased efforts should be made to explore linkages between basic theory and research in the social sciences on the one hand, and educational policy and practices on the other. Considerable knowledge exists, based on research not done in educational settings, that has potential applicability to educational institutions and their operation. Specifically, the Office of Education and private foundations should consider the establishment of certain task forces addressed to this topic. A task force might be established, for example, to explore more fully the implications of research on basic learning processes (including cognitive development) for school curricula. Similarly, a great deal of research on complex organizations may be applicable to the management of school systems and their relations with communities, and a task-force effort is desirable to bridge the social science-education gap. The kind of work advocated here has already been undertaken by several of the regional laboratories sponsored by the Office of Education, and also by the American Educational Research Association. These efforts should include a greater degree of integration with traditional social science departments in universities; and a special attempt should be made to involve individual social scientists who have never worked on educational problems per se, but whose research might have bearing on the management of school systems.

Second, alternative models of the educational process based on scientific conceptions of learning and socialization processes should be tested. How much emphasis should be placed on external as opposed to intrinsic reward systems, for example? Longitudinal research designs, coupled with systematic and coordinated modifications of curricula at all levels, are crucial to such evaluations. The long history of futile attempts to demonstrate lasting results of specific short-term programs in education underscores the importance of this point. The nation's experience with Head Start provides a good example. Possible results of the preschool program in this case appear to have been in part dissipated by the inability of schools to adapt curricula (in kindergarten, grades 1, 2, and beyond) to take advantage of any gains made by children coming out of Head Start programs, let alone to continue their acceleration.

A specific alternative to the present fragmented federally-sponsored research programs in education, for example, might look as follows: A substantial amount of money might be reallocated from available funds for an experimental model schools' program. School systems, universities, and other organizations (including, possibly, private corporations) might then apply for large-scale support to be used over a five- to ten-year period to operate an *entire* school. Terms of the grant program would stipulate that any applicant for such funds must attempt to test, over the course of the grant, a specific and coherent approach to learning. Potential recipients would thus be encouraged to specify a systemwide model of the educational process. (For example, one school system might wish to design an entire school—from kindergarten to grade six or even twelve—around the use of programed learning devices, including automated and nonautomated systems.) If a number of such systemwide experiments were funded for several years, we would at last be able to make meaningful comparisons among various educational policies and practices.

Third, education needs social science knowledge in program planning, school administration, and a host of other ways. In planning innovational programs in education, for instance, the underlying theoretical rationale should be specified. The question "Why should something work?" needs to be asked before any new program is tried out. Prior consideration of this question, for instance, might have saved a great deal of current confusion over the value of reducing class size. And the answer to it might have led school systems to incorporate curriculum revisions designed to take advantage of reduced pupil-teacher ratios, rather than expecting smaller classes per se to result in increased pupil performance—a result which subsequent research has shown unlikely.

The provision of social science consultation to school systems is particularly important as a growing number of commercial organizations enter the educational market with expensive equipment deriving from technological advances in computers, audiovisual devices, and the like. School personnel usually have neither the time nor experience to evaluate the competing claims; but, as the cost and potential impact of the new educational technology increases, so does the need for impartial evaluation and interpretation.

Finally, recent controversies involving urban school systems have dramatized the need for sophisticated leadership in the area of school-community relations. Despite pressures from community groups for a larger voice in school affairs, some large school systems have become insulated from the communities they serve. Most school administrators (not to mention school board members) are inadequately prepared for the task that in fact confronts them—to manage a large bureaucratic organization so as to insure responsiveness to the wishes of constituent communities, while at the same time realizing the potential benefits of administrative centralization. Problems arising from changes in the urban community, the growth of black nationalism, the rise of teacher organizations, and the reawakening of parent interest in the school add a new and urgent dimension to relations between the social sciences and education.

Engineering

In the roles they have played in industry, consulting, and public works development, engineers have long had needs for (and made use of) social science knowledge. New product and process developments have required economic analysis—engineers engaged in public works development, in particular, have long enjoyed fruitful interrelationships with economists. The economist's concept of consumers' surplus, for instance, was developed by the engineer Dupuit and subsequently elaborated by the economist Marshall; and work upon cost-benefit and cost-effectiveness of public investments requires interplay of economists and engineers. Industrial engineers have dealt with problems of industrial organization and man-machine relationships; and they have worked closely with psychologists in government, business, and elsewhere to assure the effective design and utilization of equipment.

But even so, there are serious limitations upon the quality and quantity of social science information so far used by engineers; and needs for social science knowledge in engineering are now increasing very rapidly:

(a) There is increasing concern about the need to choose among technological alternatives and evolve new technologies in support of broad social goals.

(b) The traditional concern with man-machine systems has broadened to include relationships between physical systems and human systems.

(c) New public works endeavors must now consider *social* cost and returns, in addition to economic cost and returns.

These changes impose new requirements upon engineering and the social sciences. In addition to developing new transportation and other physical facilities, engineers must now be concerned with such questions as how values and goals affecting system preferences are evolved, and how engineering systems are perceived and used. How the environment is perceived, for example, is a crucial problem for the analysis and improvement of environmental systems.

Many engineers perceive these needs. But perception is not enough to insure that the relevant knowledge is generated, or that it is transmitted to practicing professionals, or that it affects the training of young engineers. The time lag between the need for new knowledge and the impact of this need in the field is long, as is the lag between the generation of new knowledge and its general availability and use.

Engineers must be trained to assist better in (1) *identification* of the problems of society that merit technological solutions, and (2) the *evaluation* of the potential consequences that such solutions may have on society. This does not mean that engineers must be trained as social scientists; it *does* mean that revisions in traditional engineering curricula are called for. In particular, engineers must be given the knowledge to appreciate the relevance of social science theory to their work, as well as the ability to know what kinds of assistance social scientists can provide them.

Both engineering and social science departments must be sensitive to these needs. More time in undergraduate curricula must be devoted to training engineers in the social sciences; new types of courses and more responsive strategies and tactics for accomplishing this training are called for. For example, stronger efforts must be made to demonstrate to engineers the importance and relevance of the social sciences to engineering. This calls for careful consideration of the interfaces between the two; it will require more effective interdepartmental cooperation; it must be founded on carefully structured interactions between the social sciences and engineering, in research as well as in teaching activities.

The second promising front for improving utilization lies in collaborative attacks by social scientists and engineers on major social problems. For one thing, demands on social science coming from the activities of engineers will require some changes in social science research itself. When new technology, for instance, makes it possible to irrigate deserts, the demands on social scientists to participate in planning the most desirable new communities present a challenge to their resources.

Conversely, social science theory often delineates an approach to solving social problems that demands the development of certain technologies. The challenge to engineering technology to create devices for implementing social science solutions is growing. For instance, in the field of criminology the accumulation of research knowledge is extensive and points to the need for developing detection systems, alarm systems, new lighting designs in cities, and so on. To turn to a successful example, we note that basic learning from psychology has guided the recent engineering development of teaching machines—with consequent major changes in educational institutions.

The engagement of engineering with the social sciences leads to confrontation between conflicting public values. For instance, when technology made possible the production of the supersonic transport, social scientists were requested to devise ways to dampen the public reaction to the sonic boom. At the same time, research on psychological stress—with loud intermittent noises used as the stressor—clearly presents a challenge to engineers to search for different aircraft design that will reduce the sonic boom. When such collaboration involves conflicting public values—leading to the very live question of whether engineering is to be employed in the service of social science theory or social scientists are to find solutions to the impact of technology on society—the demands of each upon the other may well be beneficial in the long run, particularly if they lead to increasing research effort from both sides.

Journalism

The social sciences can assist the mass media in reporting current social issues in depth and putting them in context. Nevertheless, with few notable exceptions, the relationship between journalism and the social sciences has never been close. Rarely do journalists, for instance, make more than spasmodic use of available social science knowledge when reporting unrest. A school controversy may be treated as an education story when it is in fact rooted in racial discrimination or the contest for jobs. Urban riots may be reported as a protest of unemployed black members of society, when in fact the effective leadership has been supplied by the successful, upwardly mobile members of the black community. Individuals with high visibility are accepted as spokesmen for a racial or religious group when they may represent only themselves or a very tiny minority—a fact which adequate sampling according to social science procedures would readily demonstrate. (Among the notable exceptions, by way of illustration, is the reporting of the 1967 Detroit riots by one of the city's newspapers in which it fielded a large team of reporters for an in-depth survey that made effective use of social science techniques and also used social scientists as advisers.)

Responsibility for the present lack of productive relationships cannot be laid entirely at the door of the press. Increasing specialization within the social sciences has led to the growth of esoteric terminologies that are often incomprehensible to the reporter. Research techniques have become more and more difficult for a layman to understand. Many social scientists distrust the press because of its past inaccuracies, and refuse to deal with reporters, thereby insuring that inaccuracies will multiply. Most are so unfamiliar with the news media as institutions that they are unable to understand the requirements and pressures to which the journalist is subjected.

Efforts to foster communication between journalists and social scientists have been made by universities, foundations, and the news industry itself. Although these efforts have so far fallen short of meeting the need, journalism schools are increasingly incorporating elements from political science, sociology, and economics into their curricula. The Ford Foundation has supported a special urban journalism program at Northwestern University. The Columbia Broadcasting System fellowships and Stanford fellowships make it possible for journalists to study the social sciences, although other fields are open to them as well. The Nieman fellowships also provide opportunities to journalists for advanced study.[3] Several other foundation-supported programs for journalists, involving fellowships or special seminars, are provided for those who wish to increase their familiarity with the social sciences.

To date, the Columbia Broadcasting System is one of the very few news organizations to have devoted major financial resources of its own to mid-career education for its personnel; but the industry as a whole has proved increasingly willing to support fellowship and seminar programs. (More than two hundred newspapers, for instance, contributed to Harvard's campaign to match a Ford Foundation grant for expansion of the Nieman fellowships.) Nevertheless, most news organizations have failed to invest significantly in upgrading their professional staffs; some have even been reluctant to grant leaves of absence for mid-career study when another institution was paying the bill.

The media can afford to give greater support to fellowship programs, and other mechanisms through which journalists can keep abreast of social science knowledge, and the Commission urges them to do so.

In view of the accelerating rate of social change and the growing complexity of our society, the links between social science and journalism must be strengthened and increased. Steps should be taken by universities, research institutes, foundations, and other institutions doing research to make social scientists and their research findings more accessible to journalists. Similarly, it is highly desirable that news media permit and encourage more on-the-job education in the social sciences, and also allow reporters covering complicated social issues adequate time for thorough research and careful writing. Coverage of the New York public school crisis in the fall of 1968, for example, was badly hampered both by most reporters' lack of familiarity with the background of the crisis and also by frequent changes in assignment.

---

[3] An analysis of the 350 newspapermen who have held these fellowships over the past 30 years indicates that history, chiefly American history, has been a primary interest to the largest number. In the past several years, fellows have also indicated strong interest in the other social sciences.

Numerous supporting measures could be taken by foundations and universities. Journalism schools should continue to place increased emphasis on social science content; they should also teach their students how to secure specialized information from social scientists when this would assist in-depth coverage. Social science departments, for their part, should encourage their faculty members to respond positively to journalists who are trying to establish channels of communication. Faculty members, for example, should insure that their graduate students are sufficiently familiar with news media as institutions to permit worthwhile discussion with journalists. One-term courses or workshops in "journalism for social scientists" might in some cases be sponsored jointly by journalism schools and social science departments.

Professional associations could do much more to assist in the communication of relevant social science research results and thinking. The American Psychological Association has taken an important step in this direction by the establishment of a new office, one of the main functions of which is to work effectively with the profession of journalism in providing background for news coverage from psychology. The publications programs of professional associations have not provided authoritative pamphlets to inform the journalism profession on substantive issues. The associations should review the possibility of publishing a series of booklets designed to present clearly and dispassionately the knowledge gained from their profession's research on areas of vital journalistic concern—aging, violence, death, black-white relations, student unrest, addiction, etc.

Professional associations can also contribute by organizing at each annual meeting one session oriented toward the press and the general public. These sessions, consisting of papers commissioned by the association's press-relations committee, would suggest implications of selected ongoing research and thinking for specific social problems. There might well be organized, in addition, occasional sessions providing for discussion between social scientists and invited journalists on specialized subjects.

Working together, then, the news industry, universities, and foundations should insure that an adequate number of mid-career fellowships for journalists are available at selected institutions throughout the country. The same three parties should support the establishment for journalists of periodic social science seminars and briefings, organized on a regional basis. They should also cooperate in exploring new ways to explain social issues to the public. Research and experimentation in improving the utilization of television and radio for this purpose is highly desirable—action along these lines being especially necessary if the full potentialities of *public* television are to be realized.

Law

For at least half a century able men in the legal profession have recognized the potential contribution of social science to the law. For most of this period the potential has remained undeveloped. There was a strong flurry of interest (part of the "legal realist" movement) during the 1920's and 1930's, but few social science techniques or findings were actually used by lawyers. In recent years this interest has been renewed, and seems here to stay, because the issues and problems confronting our legal institutions demand more than the background typically brought to these problems by persons with traditional law school training.

This need for social science contributions is apparent both for immediate concrete problems facing the nation, and also for more basic areas of inquiry into the functioning of law and legal institutions. With regard to the former, consider the following illustrative problems:

In tort law, the problem of compensation for accident victims. The best work in this area surely requires a solid understanding of economics, since many of the alternative proposals for reforming the system of compensation rest heavily on assumptions regarding their differing economic impact. The different plans for accident compensation are also based on differing psychological assumptions regarding the behavior of people, thus requiring an important contribution to be made by psychologists.

The utilization of legal institutions in developing countries. Legal institutions may be used as a lever for intended social and economic change. Programs designed to foster such change require knowledge about the relationship between law and other institutions in developing societies. Contributions from anthropologists and sociologists, as well as from specialists in comparative government, are badly needed.

Labor law, and the problem of how far labor relations should be "judicialized" and handled through the courts. This problem area requires a background in administrative science and industrial economics.

The effects of Supreme Court decisions on the administration of criminal justice. Decisions designed to insure the rights of defendants are felt by some to hamper unduly the police and other law enforcement agencies in their efforts to control delinquency and crime. Such claims are important, if true, and it is possible to design empirical research to provide evidence as to whether they are true or not.

The problem of a heavy backlog of cases in both our civil and criminal courts. Systematic studies of the court process and of the flow of cases through various stages of litigation may point the way to changes designed to make the courts more efficient with no sacrifice in justice or fairness.

These are only a few examples of how the social sciences can be relevant to our understanding of immediate, concrete problems facing our legal institutions. There is a similar need in the development of basic knowledge about legal institutions and their functioning in society. Social scientists who have studied the professions are equipped to examine the changing role of the legal profession. Those who have made their focus of inquiry the study of large-scale formal organizations have much to contribute to our knowledge about the effects of law schools on their students. Social psychologists who study the socialization process may provide an understanding of the way persons develop conceptions of justice and fairness. The tools of survey research can be applied fruitfully to studying the public's experience with lawyers and legal institutions.

A number of different programs are already making a contribution. The National Science Foundation is now authorized to support scientific studies in the area of law. The National Institute of Mental Health has supported research studies that link law and social science, and has also provided support for lawyers to receive training in the behavioral sciences. The National Institute of Law Enforcement and Criminal Justice may support sociolegal studies within the criminal justice area, and the Office of Economic Opportunity has provided the same kind of support through the Institute for Research on Poverty.

Programs outside the federal government include those sponsored by a number of philanthropic foundations. Several university-based training programs designed to provide interdisciplinary training for both lawyers and social scientists have been established by the Russell Sage Foundation. The Walter E. Meyer Research Institute is devoted to studies of legal institutions that often include a social science component. The Ford Foundation has provided large-scale support for demonstration and research programs in the area of criminal justice. The American Bar Foundation has undertaken a number of empirical research projects designed to shed light on the functioning of specific legal institutions. Applied research studies of the courts and related agencies have been undertaken by The RAND Corporation and similar organizations. Finally, the growing interest of law schools in providing both social science training and research is concretely reflected in the growing number of appointments of social scientists to law school faculties.

All these programs offer promise for the long-term development of social science contributions to our understanding of legal institutions. The most important single fact, however, is that most of these programs are of recent origin and their total amount of financial support remains small. American law schools, with limited exceptions, have been and remain largely professional training centers rather than centers for the development and advance of knowledge about the *operation* of law and legal institutions. And the various social science disciplines have devoted only marginal attention to these problems. We know far too little, therefore, about one of the basic institutions in our society.

What can be done to develop further knowledge about the operation of legal institutions, or to make better utilization of the knowledge we now have? The Commission recommends three related programs:

First, there is a need for programs designed to improve both public and professional understanding of the relationships between law and social science. Such programs can encourage both law schools and social science departments to develop substantial interdisciplinary training. At the moment there are only the barest beginnings of programs that provide either training in the social science disciplines for legal scholars, or training in law for social scientists. Yet both groups need a much deeper understanding of the problems and the capabilities of the other if they are to work together effectively in efforts to produce useful knowledge.

The need extends far beyond the few scholars who may be doing specific empirical studies of legal institutions. If lawyers are to function effectively as professionals and in the community, they will need to be familiar with social science findings and concepts. Law schools do provide opportunities for such training in the second and third years; but they may well require special inducements if they are to move into these areas with a greater sense of purpose and direction. Similarly, since it is conspicuous that even the best-educated segment of our population knows relatively little about the operation of legal institutions, materials and courses on law and legal institutions should be developed for nonlawyers. There is surely a place for such courses in a well-rounded liberal arts education. Again, because of the relative insulation of the law schools from undergraduate education, such efforts are not likely to develop in any important way without concerted attention and leadership.

Second, there is a central need for policy-oriented knowledge regarding the social and economic effects of a variety of different legal arrangements. Every law, every appellate court decision, every administrative procedure, has an underlying set of assumptions about how people act and how their actions can be controlled. Lawyers obviously know what the legal forms are, and they have rich ideas as to how they should be changed; but they are not equipped, as a rule, to study in detail the actual impact of different legal arrangements. Providing systematic answers requires expertise in sampling, survey design, and analysis of statistical data. Social science studies designed to test these assumptions, and to determine clearly the different social and economic effects of various legal procedures and rulings, therefore, are urgently needed.

The range and variety of problems in sociolegal research precludes any easy or simple method for implementing this recommendation. (1) Existing centers and institutes might, in some cases, serve as the major vehicle for further development and use of social science. (2) In other instances, the new social problem research institutes recommended by the Commission would serve the purpose. (3) Policy-oriented governmental commissions and agencies addressing legal problems might benefit from having social scientists as staff members. (4) Finally, because of the range and possible overlap of contributions, special coordinative mechanisms informed of the total range of sociolegal research efforts may have to be developed.

Third, we need basic research on the place of law in society, the social conditions under which legal processes emerge and change, and the broad social consequences of these changes. Support for basic research in law-related areas is just as necessary as in other scientific fields. Such research may cover the whole range from descriptive empirical studies to theoretical efforts in jurisprudence.

This goal should be achieved so that it stresses the social science dimension of legal study. To this end it is important that such basic research be interdisciplinary and *not* established as a separate and isolated program of legal studies. It is equally important, however, that legally trained people also participate. Such a program could be organized, for example, within the social science division of the National Science Foundation. A program administered by the NSF could, in addition to providing direct support for social science studies of the legal process, also provide funds for the types of training programs outlined in the first recommendation. Finally, such a program should be defined broadly enough to include those scholarly studies of law conducted by legal scholars (as distinct from social scientists), but which make significant use of social science writings and materials. All of these programs could be administered through committees (composed of both legal scholars and social scientists) designed to evaluate grant proposals for training, scholarship, and research.

Medicine and Public Health

Medicine and public health, though closely and inextricably interwoven, are not interchangeable. While medicine serves and contributes to public health, the health of the public is also protected and restored to a large extent by nonmedical measures.

The relationship between social factors and the health of the public has been recognized since antiquity. Society has traditionally undertaken community-wide efforts to protect, restore, and maintain its health—whether through ritual sacrifices, prayers, heroic measures to stop pestilences, quarantine, massive immunization campaigns, community controls to purify water supplies, or federal financing of a general hospital system. In recent years, the public health profession and the government have become much more concerned with providing health services to the underprivileged not only to control chronic diseases and environmental hazards once they have appeared, but also to use the wisdom and logic of preventive health practice *before* the fact. The contribution of the social sciences has thus become clearly relevant because preventive health practice depends on the ability to influence such things as individual and community attitudes and motivations; life patterns; the priorities for individual and community spending; and organizational change.

The following discussion is not exhaustive or complete. It merely illustrates the dependence of public health and medical progress upon social science research. This need has been partially recognized during the past two decades. We must now greatly extend those research efforts, and adopt programs that will focus directly upon implementing the insights, knowledge, and techniques emerging from them.

An individual may not notice, or if he notices he may not recognize, or if he recognizes he may still not accept the fact that a certain change in function may be a sign of illness, perhaps even serious, which could be treated and cured. He may fear the diagnosis because of resulting treatment costs or possible effects on his future life. Alternatively, he may not be able to obtain care or he may not know where it is available to him. All these factors and considerations exercise a direct and profound influence upon his participation in and benefit from the medical care system. The study and understanding of those perceptions and characteristics of the people to be served is an obvious task for sociology, anthropology, economics, and social psychology. Those fields are well established. Much useful information, not yet fully utilized, is already available; and greater knowledge, when put to use, can clearly be expected to improve our health services system.

The study of the technical and professional component of the medical care complex—the people, programs, and institutions providing medical care—is also largely dependent upon the application of the knowledge, theory, skills, and methods of the social sciences. The vast quantity of biological knowledge applicable to medical care, and the rapid rate of accumulation of new knowledge in recent decades, have led perforce to increasing specialization. And this has occurred not only in the medical and nursing professions. Many totally new professions and technologies have been developed, each with its own goals, techniques, and responsibilities. The optimal involvement of all such personnel cries out for a working context of teamwork which barely exists in this, or any other, country.

Present-day knowledge and national expectations, as mentioned above, require that medical care be defined broadly enough to encompass the complete range of personal health services—from the promotion of health and the prevention or early detection of disease through to the diagnosis, treatment, *and* rehabilitation of the patient. In America today, the principle has been widely accepted that this full range of protective and restorative services should be available to all our citizens regardless of their geographic location or their social station. Given the armory of biological knowledge now available, our crucial task is to apply it fully, effectively, and economically.

This task has enormous implications for the training of doctors and allied professions, but it is also clearly a task for the social sciences. We are dealing here with a series of interrelated components which together make up the medical care complex. These components fall into three groups: (1) people needing services; (2) people, programs, and institutions providing services; and (3) the organized arrangements for performing medical care functions. The shape, form, and function of each of these components —and the interactions within and among them—determine the cost, acceptability, and effectiveness of the process as a whole.

1. It is well known that people have widely differing concepts of their medical care needs. Only a small proportion of our population has the sophistication, motivation, and means to perceive medical care as one of a broad range of services which should be available for their appropriate use. For many, medical care is a service sought only when an undesirable illness or injury interferes with their normal abilities, functions, or activities. And what is considered "normal" and to be expected is known to vary widely, within communities, by social class.

2. In recent years, particularly since the passage and implementation of Medicare and Medicaid, our medical care system has come under increasing scrutiny. The rapidly mounting cost of medical care has puzzled, dismayed, frustrated, and even angered

more and more sections of the community—individuals, agencies, community leaders, and government officials.

The scarcity of medical and allied personnel, both in rural areas and in the slum districts of our cities, coupled with the inadequacy of the range and quantity of institutional programs and facilities virtually everywhere, has been highlighted by the recent broad national steps to begin removing the economic barriers preventing much of our population from obtaining the medical care they need. Poignancy is added to the dissatisfaction with our health services system by the frequent manifestations of inadequate attention by medical care personnel, programs, and institutions, to the vital human aspécts of their day-to-day, hour-to-hour, person-to-person activities and relationships with the patients and community they serve.

These serious defects, which will undoubtedly come under increasing public scrutiny, are not an expression of deficiencies of the scientific biological technology of medical care. They are clearly an expression of deficiencies in its societal, organizational, and behavioral technology. Social science insight and research are basic to an understanding of the role relationships of all the members of the health team; to their setting of goals; and to the organization and administration of their total effort at all levels.

In the provision of service the individuals, the programs, and the institutions are all directly affected in orientation, operation, cost, and effectiveness by an interwoven series of factors. Professional goals; values and expectations; methods of remuneration; economic, functional, and service characteristics; behavior patterns and influences; the nature and opportunities for professional and economic advancement—these are but a few examples. An encouraging, though small, start has been made in the development and conduct of relevant research; but implementation of the knowledge and the insight thereby acquired has, thus far, been slight and very uneven.

3. The third major component of the medical care complex—the arrangements for performing the health service functions—is the social nexus linking the first two. It embraces not only the personal and professional goals of providers and recipients, but also a broad and pervasive range of socially oriented objectives and procedures developed by the community, the state, and the nation.

The proportion of the total national product being spent for health services has been climbing in the past decade until it has now reached the level of 6.5 per cent, one of the highest in the world. At the same time that we are adopting the principle of equality of opportunity for health services, the fund of biological knowledge to be applied in medical care has vastly increased.

Social science research and information on the methods of applying this biological knowledge, however, are far behind the progress in biology. In the field of health services our technology has far outstripped our service delivery. Progress toward a more rational organization of health services has been slow and halting. Social science research, followed by the implementation of its findings, is fundamental to decisive and direct movement in this direction. Sole practice in an era of highly specialized science; filling the gap in services available in our slums and rural areas; continuous, humane, and restorative care to our aged and chronic sick; lifting prevention of disease to its proper position of primacy; raising the level of technological sophistication of the public (and especially the minority groups) about health and health services; achieving meaningful coordination of hospital and health programs and the many other autonomous health agencies in a region; implementing innovation and resolving the social and professional conflicts that inevitably arise—all these, clearly, are problems for social science. (While due involvement of health personnel and the relevant health services is, of course, also crucial, they provide the context rather than point to the solution.) In the past fifteen years a start has been made through the establishment of research efforts—largely sociological—in such medical settings as medical schools, hospitals, and health departments. This needs to be greatly expanded in both scope and volume.

The social sciences have already made a basic contribution in yet another, and quite different, field of medicine and public health—the study and elucidation of the role of social factors in the etiology and natural history of certain disease processes. There is increasing evidence that many disease processes involve an interaction between characteristics of man's internal body systems (physiological, biochemical, anatomical, etc.) on the one hand; and, on the other, his external physical environment, personality or psychological characteristics, social experiences, his standard of living, level of educational attainment, and the forces of culture and attitudes under which he lives.

Such interaction has not always been adequately heeded in the training of physicians, despite studies demonstrating the important effect of social factors in certain diseases. Tuberculosis has long been known to be more common in the lower socioeconomic classes than in the higher. Coronary heart disease has been recently shown a more common cause of death in certain occupational and socioeconomic groups than in others.

To take another example: In Western Europe, Scandinavia, and the English-speaking countries, an extensive change in the distribution of peptic ulcer in the population has taken place. In the late nineteenth century, this disease was more prevalent among females than males. Today the ratio has been reversed. Is this due to the extensive changes in the family in these countries, and to the changes in the roles of women and men in society and in relationship to each other? Another puzzling social problem is presented by the fact that mortality from gastric ulcer is the highest in the lowest social classes, while mortality from duodenal ulcer is highest in the highest social class.

We are coming, therefore, to the realization that for many of mankind's most important diseases in modern industrialized society there is not a single cause. For this concept to be fully exploited, research must be stimulated which will focus upon the interplay between social, psychological, and physical environment, and internal biological body mechanisms. For many important diseases the limitations of clinical and experimental laboratory approaches to the study of causation can be overcome by epidemiological studies—the occurrence of the disease in populations—which give visibility to the multiplicity of causative agents by paying adequate attention to social factors.

The political, economic, and social influences on health control and health promotion measures are strong and important. For example, the large-scale reduction in dental caries in growing children who live in areas served by a water supply that has been fluoridated is well known. It has been a source of surprise, disappointment, and frustration to the dental profession and to public health departments to see the opposition to this community-wide measure develop in many communities where this measure has been debated and decided by the public. The social characteristics of the vigorous and often victorious opposition to this measure have been subjected to research. More research is needed if more effective programs of environmental control are to be implemented.[4] Or again: The close association of cigarette smoking with cancer of the lung has convinced public health authorities that cigarette smoking should be curbed; but efforts to do so have thus far not been notably successful. If we are to develop more effective measures of social control we must research further a wide range of interacting social-behavioral-economic forces.

Recent growth of interest in the problem of environmental pollution—in the fact that our skies and our rivers have in many places become veritable sewers—also highlights the fact that the lessons of physical and biological science do not of themselves point to the patterning of adequate and acceptable health protec-

---

[4] Or alternative forms of fluoridation must be developed that can be implemented privately.

tion programs. Pittsburgh was the first large city in the United States to tackle the problem of air pollution in an overall, community-wide, effective manner. It is almost two decades since this demonstration took place. Yet very few cities have followed suit on the same scale. The explanation is to be found, not in the relevant physical and biological facts, but rather in the social, economic, and political situation.

Mental Health Work

As in the larger field of health and medicine generally, relationships between social factors and mental health or disorder have long been recognized. Until recently, however, there has been less clear recognition that the effectiveness of mental health programs and services is to a very high degree dependent upon social and cultural factors. Unlike other illnesses, mental disorders are often not recognized as such either by the person afflicted or by those near and dear to him. Mental disorders disrupt the shared understandings that make social life possible; frequently they lead to hostility and conflict between the ill person and those family members and friends who would be most supportive and sympathetic if he were physically ill. Therefore, the social context in which mental illness is defined and responded to takes on special significance.

Further, what is called mental disorder includes a heterogeneous group of behaviors and mental or emotional states—some reflecting the psychological effects of organic disease or genetic constitution; some being reactions to intense psychological stress; some representing inadequate or maladaptive personal strategies; and some constituting deviant modes of behaving, thinking, and feeling that are common or at least frequent among members of particular segments of the population. It is now widely recognized that mental health cannot be divorced from position within the society. The Supreme Court acted on the matter of school desegregation when it was no longer possible to doubt that segregation was psychologically damaging to the excluded population. With the advent of large-scale surveys of the epidemiology—usually collaborative ventures involving psychiatrists and social scientists—we find a very high relationship between the symptoms of mental disorder and deprivation, and alienation from the goals of the larger society. Promising as such leads are for a more adequate understanding of the nature of mental disorder, there is a vast need for more detailed and precise studies by teams that bring together expert clinicians and social scientists—the latter group including not only social psychologists, sociologists, and anthropologists already involved, but also economists and political scientists.

Some recent epidemiological studies indicate so high a prevalence of symptoms of mental disorder in the general population as to suggest that direct therapeutic intervention on an individual basis is unrealistic except for the more severely ill or those likely to become disabled in the absence of any such intervention. Moreover, a certain level of tension (with resulting symptoms) is an almost inevitable consequence of life in a complex society. The task is to assess the optimal level of services to be provided within the society as a whole, and the nature of services most meaningful and effective in particular segments of the population.

Despite considerable public education in the past two decades, and some real improvement in public attitudes toward mental illness and psychiatric services, mental disorder still carries a stigma in large parts of the population; and psychiatry is not yet perceived as a potential source of help, but remains a threat to many persons. Moreover, it is apparent that psychiatric techniques and approaches that are helpful with people who are verbally fluent and given to examining their feelings may be quite useless with those whose way of life does not include either of these attributes. One of the contributions of social science has been to point up the distinctions between what community members define as inappropriate and deviant behavior, and the identification of persons as mentally ill.

Severe mental illness still entails hospitalization for protracted periods for some persons, and short-term hospital stays for many. It is not accidental that the first significant decline in the number of patients in the mental hospitals of the United States for extended periods was preceded by research that demonstrated how the practice of incarcerating patients in large, isolated mental hospitals was rendering individuals unfit to live in normal society. Among patients hospitalized continuously for two or more years, only a tiny proportion ever again managed to return to independent life in the community.

Many factors have contributed to the decline in our mental hospital population during the past decade—better staffing, tranquilizing drugs, changed administrative policies, greater allocation of responsibilities to patients, greater attention to the patient's ties outside the hospital—but most of them have built upon the increased understanding both of the mental hospital as a social institution and of the relationship between institutional processes and the well-being of the individual patient. A relatively small number of studies has had a major impact, and one may anticipate that the time will come when every treatment facility will periodically examine its mode of operation from the varied perspectives of those it serves.

The use of the social milieu of the hospital as a therapeutic instrument is not a new idea, but the systematic study of how to make that milieu most therapeutic for different kinds of patients, and how best to prepare the patient for the transition back to the community, has barely begun. New kinds of facilities—day hospitals, night hospitals, "halfway houses"—are being developed in recognition of the need to keep the patient as fully anchored in the community and in normal life roles as is possible for him. The planning of such facilities increasingly involves social scientists, as does the effort to evaluate their effectiveness. Although there are many complexities in the evaluation of the new community mental health program, social science research methods provide at least a potential means for assessing their efficacy and cost benefits.

Psychology has been a key contributor to the growth and development of mental health. The role and contribution of clinical psychology is well known; and includes both broad scientific research and psychological test construction on the one hand, and professional work in psychodiagnosis and psychotherapy on the other. New therapies, such as techniques of behavior modification, have been pioneered to a significant degree by clinical psychologists. Members of this branch of psychology have also played a leading role in the development of systematic methods for assessing the mental health status of patients, both as a contribution to psychodiagnostics and as a means of gauging the progress of patients under various regimes of treatment.

Mental health workers now generally recognize that early detection of the symptoms and signs of serious mental disorders and appropriate intervention can often short-circuit the course of pathology and avoid the necessity of removing the patient from the community. Not only have the out-patient services markedly increased in recent years, but there has been a pronounced trend toward developing community mental health centers that will bring therapeutic and consultative services into local areas and institutions. Quite clearly there is no one pattern of services that will meet the needs of rural areas, suburbs, and central cities. As already noted, the meaning of mental disorder and the responses made to mental disorder are largely determined by views prevailing in segments of the society or community. Knowledge of subcultural beliefs and practices and of the dynamics of power and prestige in the local community become prerequisite to effective planning and development of services. It appears quite likely that new specialties will be evolved to meet such needs, perhaps combining social science skills with training in clinical psychiatry and psychology.

Because mental disorder so frequently incapacitates the individual for substantial periods of time, the economic costs of mental illness are exceptionally high. So likewise are the costs of treatment, which explains the much greater public role in providing mental (as opposed to physical) health services and facilities. Insurance programs are increasingly coming into being. Public policy in this area will be heavily dependent for sound data on research by economists and specialists in public administration.

The concerns of the field of mental health and its specialists overlap considerably with those of social work. Mental disorders are frequently associated with other forms of deviant behavior—alcoholism, drug addiction, delinquency, and the like—that are even more sharply related to environmental pressures and group patterns. In these areas of concern, little understanding either of the problems themselves or of the possible means of dealing with them can be achieved without a comprehension of the social matrix in which they are found.

The circumstances of the broad profession of mental health are particularly favorable for effective linkage between social science knowledge and significant social problems. Behavioral and social scientists often work side-by-side with practitioners, with research being conducted in the very settings where services are being performed. Thus, excellent opportunities are afforded for planned involvement of practitioners in the stimulation of research and emphasis on selected problems. Because of the interrelationship between the conditions of social life and mental illness, the fields of social psychiatry and preventive psychiatry require a broad understanding of social science knowledge. From the perspective of this report, the mental health field and the federal programs in mental health represent a major resource for direct utilization of social science knowledge and techniques.

Social Work

Since early in the present century when social work began to emerge as a profession, its activities have been increasingly based on knowledge from the social sciences. Its earliest focus on the amelioration of personal problems has led it inexorably to concern for the improvement of social conditions. The industrialization and urbanization of America; mass immigrations; recurrent economic disorders; and the persistence of racial conflict and poverty in a mass society—these are among the conditions impelling the profession's attention to the social forces that shape human development and life.

Most social work practitioners have been employed in a broad range of voluntary and public agencies providing services to persons with problems. These responsibilities have understandably emphasized professional reliance on that social science theory having direct import for individual behavior, especially contributions from the discipline of psychology. Social work turned initially to the individual psychologies of the early twentieth century, and later to Freudian theory and derivative psychoanalytic and clinical concepts.

In the first decades of this century, the agency-connected training programs for preparing social work personnel began a movement toward the universities. These educational programs, although sometimes part of or closely connected with an academic department such as sociology, more often became early established as separate graduate professional schools. They tended to remain apart from the main disciplines and developments within the academic community. Many of the early leaders in social work education were social scientists—most commonly from sociology, economics, and political science—and they taught courses in some schools during these years. Very few of these social scientists had their major academic affiliation as faculty members of schools of social work, unless (as many did) they became deans of the schools.

Because most practitioners were located in agencies providing interpersonal services, social work and its educational programs became heavily infused with the perspectives of psychological theories. These provided substantive knowledge about behavior having greatest salience to social workers, including the processes of human development and the etiology of personal problems. Because psychoanalytic theory in particular offered clear prescriptions for professional intervention, and presented few problems in transformation, it had special utility in guiding practitioner-client interactions. To a lesser extent other kinds of knowledge were also useful in providing understanding of the varieties of human behavior under different cultural conditions, and of the socioeconomic conditions that shape behavior and experience. The latter included contributions from social stratification, family sociology, race and ethnic relations, social disorganization and deviance, and so on.

The development, in the early 1930's, of group work—as another method in social work in addition to casework—led to the use of ideas from recreation and progressive education and to greater use of learning theory in social work education. Similarly the development within social work of community organization, and its rapid growth in the last two decades, has increased the need for and use of all the social sciences—with special focus on political science, concepts of social stratification, and organization theory.

This brief analysis provides a historical picture of social science knowledge resources that have been drawn upon and the ways these have been put to use in a profession which was at first primarily oriented to behavior at the individual level. Substantive work that addressed individual behavior directly had greatest relevance (i.e., psychological and social psychological theory). Next, knowledge that most immediately yielded intervention methods, or that could most easily lead to prescriptions for action, was the most rapidly assimilated. In the past two decades learning theory and work in the area of behavioral modification has found an increasingly receptive audience within the profession. Knowledge that provides understanding of the more distant forces shaping human life and generating individual problems has also been drawn upon, but less fully. Cultural anthropology, for example, is among the resources that have been utilized in this more tenuous way.

Despite an early preoccupation with service to individuals, social work never relinquished its concern with social forces that seem to generate personal troubles. Efforts during the Depression of the 1930's and the establishment of the social security system in which social work was a prime mover, drew largely on concepts from economics and public administration. The direction of effort shifted in the period following World War II, as the profession began to explore problems of urbanization in a way different from its earlier concern with the allocation and coordination of social services at the local level. Sociological studies of the community—and particularly of community power and conflict—were among the first to be drawn upon as the profession expanded its urban interests and changed its emphasis. The descriptive clarity of these lines of work, and the readiness with which they could yield community action strategies, facilitated use of such contributions. Beginning about 1960, professional concern was revitalized by the launching of national social welfare and related programs (i.e., comprehensive juvenile delinquency programs, comprehensive community mental health centers). Declaration of the "war on poverty" served as a dramatic stimulus in focusing the profession's attention on problems of poverty, of the ghetto and urban decay, of discrimination and race conflict, and of inadequate health and welfare services. The knowledge base available to address these matters was, of course, wholly inadequate. A variety of efforts was initiated to promote the development of the social science knowledge base of social work and to solicit contributions from social scientists that could assist in comprehending these problems and in devising means for their resolution.

Political science, urban planning, law, "welfare economics," the study of social movements, race and ethnic relations, administrative science, and political sociology are among the resources utilized in the early twentieth century to which the profession returned. Within a relatively short span of years, social scientists from these areas have begun to teach in graduate schools of social work, although often retaining their primary anchorage in academic departments. Such persons have been encouraged to deliver papers at professional conferences, and to codify their knowledge in the form of literature. Special conferences and publications of the Council on Social Work Education, and of the National Association of Social Workers, have provided means for rapid and extensive dissemination of such material.

Several more or less independent trends have contributed to these developments and allow some estimations of their future course. Professional schools of social work have been gradually drawn toward more central geographical locations within the academic community, thus reducing their isolation from the university's major influences. The proliferation of social welfare programs of all kinds has been accompanied by an extended deployment of professional personnel; within these newer contexts professionals have assumed responsibilities beyond those directed primarily at service to individuals, and have needed to enlarge their knowledge base accordingly. The greatest expansion of the knowledge resources of the social sciences has also occurred during this period —with a gradual rise in policy orientations and in willingness to attend directly to social problems, programs, and issues. The last trend is perhaps the most significant, since it has yielded knowledge more directly relevant to the tasks of the profession, and in forms which pose fewer problems of translation or transformation.

The integration of social science and social practice, and the assimilation of knowledge into professional education, has been deliberately fostered by several endeavors affecting many graduate schools. Federal agencies—spearheaded by the National Institute of Mental Health—have initiated funding programs to support the training of social scientists and, more especially, doctoral programs for the advanced education of social workers. At the same time, these agencies have expanded support for research programs through which the knowledge and methodology of the social sciences can be brought to bear on problems relevant to social policy and practice. The Russell Sage Foundation first provided direct support to stimulate and advance the integration of social science within the graduate faculties of social work schools, as part of a larger endeavor directed at several professions. Additionally, several journals have been launched that are designed to facilitate the assimilation and application of social science contributions to social practice.

The Council on Social Work Education has exerted a major influence both in providing resources for dissemination of social science knowledge and in expanding and intensifying the use of such knowledge. Illustrative publications, generally based on special conferences, include *Social Science in the Professional Education of Social Workers* (1958); *Concepts of Prevention and Control: Their Use in the Social Work Curriculum* (1961); *The Socio-Behavioral Approach and Applications to Social Work* (1967); and *The General Systems Approach: Contributions Toward an Holistic Conception of Social Work* (1969). An extensive program in relation to developing undergraduate education in social welfare seeks to attract to the profession young people with a sound underpinning in one of the social sciences and, simultaneously, to discourage development of too narrowly technical an emphasis. Most undergraduate programs in social welfare are part of interdisciplinary programs or sociology departments, and the faculty is generally composed of sociologists.

Recruitment and development of faculty and stimulation of curriculum development in graduate and undergraduate programs are all directed toward maximizing the utilization of social science materials in relation to social welfare programs. CSWE's institutes, seminars, and annual program meetings for a number of years have emphasized the relevance of social science concepts and theories to the development of social work theory and method. A major three-year curriculum study of community organization (to be completed in 1969) draws heavily on various models from the social sciences in presenting proposals for a comprehensive curriculum to prepare for work in community planning and action programs.

Despite these encouraging developments, several barriers and problems have retarded progress. There are still too few well-trained social scientists willing to assume full-time teaching positions in the professional schools, partly because of limitations in the total ranks of such persons, and partly because of reluctance to move into situations that seem removed from the mainstream of their disciplines. Although eighteen United States schools of social work have inaugurated doctoral programs for the advanced education of social workers, the total number of graduates[5] is far less than the demand for such persons in operating programs, government agencies, and professional school faculties. Generally, these doctoral programs require basic and advanced social science courses to be taken in other academic departments on a cognate basis—even though an increasing number of social scientists is to be found among the ranks of their full-time faculty assigned to advanced studies. Given the general trends and pressures previously detailed, however, it seems likely that these patterns could be radically changed in a short time, if sufficient manpower and budgetary resources were made available. Since the graduate schools continue to be among the most potent influences on the entire profession, the quantity and quality of their faculties and the breadth and depth of their curricula will have major ramifying effects upon the profession as a whole.

The rapidly escalating problems of urban America, the persistence of widespread poverty in an affluent society, and the demands of disadvantaged minorities are creating urgent needs for social change. The knowledge of the social sciences should be among the resources readily available to the social work profession as it is called upon to assist in formulating public policy, in creating and staffing more viable programs, and in designing effective service-delivery systems. Such needs demand an expansion and even a redirection among the social sciences, since it is fair to say that we have as yet far too little reliable knowledge.

But our previous discussion suggests that mere enlargement in social science theory and knowledge will not be sufficient to meet contemporary needs. Additional efforts are required to derive from this knowledge policy and programmatic alternatives. Graduate professional schools are only one of the potential channels for pursuit of these tasks. The development of research and demonstration centers, perhaps midway between academia and the urban community, is to be encouraged. The full participation of social scientists in program design and implementation should also be encouraged. Support should be enlarged for "research-and-development" or "social engineering" approaches, which can bring social research more directly to bear on social practice, and accrue benefits already gained through analogous processes in the health sciences and industry.

---

[5] There were only 65 in 1968, the latest year for which information is available.

Much greater attention should be given in the social sciences, especially sociology and political science, to the processes of social innovation and change. We need to know a great deal more, for example, about the resistances to change in American public attitudes which impede adoption of social legislation or public programs already in effect among many Western nations. We need to know how large departments operating within the urban community can be coordinated so that their programs are mutually reinforcing rather than obstructing each other. And we need to know how human service organizations can maintain flexibility and responsiveness to shifting demands of changing populations. These exemplify the level and kinds of knowledge required by a profession whose practitioners are no longer restricted to the provision of individual services. They also are suggestive of the likely themes for inquiry among the social sciences in a changing mass society.

IV

THE SOCIAL SCIENCES AND THE FEDERAL GOVERNMENT

The Social Sciences at the White House and Departmental Level

At those levels in the federal government where major policy is made, social scientists should be deeply involved. Policies for handling the nation's most pressing issues and problems—whether they relate to the cities, pollution, inflation, or supersonic transport —must rest not only on knowledge drawn from the physical and biological sciences, but also on the best available knowledge about human individual and social behavior. Many of our most urgent policy issues, indeed, are more closely related to the social sciences and the humanities than to the natural sciences. And in these areas of federal policy-making the social sciences must be treated, not in isolation, but in their proper position as a part of the entire national pool of scientific and technological knowledge and skill.

Almost all complex public problems cut across disciplines. Virtually any contemporary federal program will serve as illustration. We seek to reduce the sulfur oxides in the air of our cities and soon find ourselves involved not only with (1) physics, (2) chemistry, and (3) engineering but also with the (4) economics of the coal mining industry in West Virginia, (5) our international relations with oil-supplying nations like Venezuela, (6) the relation of air purity to bronchitis, (7) the psychological effects of reduced or increased sunlight on behavior, and (8) the pattern of local government authorities in metropolitan areas.

Partial policies, based upon some narrow band within the whole spectrum of relevant knowledge, may cause more indirect harm

51

than direct good, and will always require costly modification, improvisation, and patching when unexpected and unwanted effects appear. We need only mention insecticides, irrigation, mass transport, and urban housing to bring to mind a host of striking examples of the pitfalls of narrow approaches to broad problems.

It follows from the interdisciplinary nature of national problems and programs that the central science policy agencies of the federal government need to span all the sciences—physical, biological, and social. The most important of these central agencies are the National Science Foundation, the Office of Science and Technology, the President's Science Advisory Committee, and the Federal Council on Science and Technology.[1]

The recent explicit inclusion (by legislation) of the social sciences within the scope of the National Science Foundation's program is another step along a long road of development. What we need now is for Congress to provide the funds, and for the NSF to move vigorously to implement its plans to expand and strengthen its program in the social sciences.

The National Academy of Sciences' recent report on *The Behavioral Sciences and the Federal Government*[2] contains a number of recommendations for the strengthening of social science participation in federal policy-making where science is involved. We concur, in general, in these recommendations, but shall elaborate on several of them.

The President's Science Advisory Committee, mostly concerned in its early years with physics (high energy physics, space research, military technology), has steadily expanded its work into (1) the other physical sciences, (2) biology, and (3) the social sciences; and, with some time lag, has gradually accepted a wider variety of scientists among its members as new kinds of scientific knowledge became relevant to its deliberations. Its membership still (as of January, 1969) contains a very high percentage of physicists, but in 1968, for the first time, a social scientist did become a member of PSAC.

In the report on *The Behavioral Sciences and the Federal Government*, mentioned above, eleven reports issued by PSAC in recent years are listed (page 86) where the relevance of social science knowledge is large and patent. In the appointment of the panels

---

[1] The comments that follow apply with equal force to the National Academy of Sciences and the National Research Council, which, though not strictly speaking federal agencies, are important national institutions for science policy. It is our view, in brief, that the social sciences are now satisfactorily incorporated in the formal National Research Council structure, but are inadequately recognized in the structure and membership of the Academy. We note with approval that the Academy's Committee on Science and Public Policy now includes several members drawn from the social sciences.

[2] *Op. cit.*, 9–12, 78–90.

that made these studies, PSAC showed a gradually growing awareness of the need to include social scientists, and the number of such panel members has grown steadily.

This trend must be continued and encouraged. Similarly, prompt recognition of the social science knowledge that should be available to PSAC itself calls for a continuation of the new policy of appointing social scientists to membership, and for increasing the number of its social science members to at least three.

The presence of social scientists on PSAC will also increase the ability of that body to recognize at an early date new scientific and technological problems that have an important social science component. For example, PSAC has played only a minor role in the assessment of the implications of computers and automation for our society. One aspect of the problem was addressed by a special Presidential Commission (independent of PSAC), and another by a PSAC panel on privacy, but the full range of problems arising out of the "information revolution" is still not squarely on the federal science policy agenda. A social scientist might well have directed attention earlier to this problem.

What has been said about the need for social science participation in PSAC applies equally to the professional staff of the Office of Science and Technology. Here, progress has been slower; no appointments of social scientists have yet been made. While able staff members drawn from the natural sciences have given vigorous and intelligent assistance to panels dealing with such topics as the development of the behavioral sciences, and educational research and development, the Commission recommends that professional social scientists with backgrounds in relevant areas be added to, and become an important part of, the OST staff.

The role of the social sciences in the Federal Council on Science and Technology presents a slightly different problem, since its membership is *ex officio*—consisting of the principal scientific officers in the several federal departments and agencies. In agencies where the physical sciences play the dominant role, the representatives will be physical scientists or engineers; in biology-based agencies, biological scientists; and in predominantly "social" agencies, social scientists. Perhaps the natural evolution in the use of science in federal departments and agencies (and the extension to all agencies of the position of Assistant Secretary for Science and Technology, or its equivalent) will lead to a balanced pattern of this sort for the FCST as a whole. Nevertheless, the social sciences have had few members on the Council in the past, and consideration should be given to drawing several such members, on an interim basis, from such bureau-level organizations as the National

Institute of Mental Health, the Office of Education, or the Census Bureau.

The Commission recognizes the current interest in establishing a Council of Social Advisers in the White House Office, to serve an advisory role parallel to that of the Council of Economic Advisers. Although we strongly agree that social science data should be fully and effectively transmitted to the administration, we are not prepared to recommend the establishment of such a council. We have become convinced that this goal can be achieved more efficiently as set forth above, by the inclusion of appropriate social scientists in such key advisory groups as PSAC and OST.

At least one top-level federal policy agency today is almost exclusively a social science domain—the Council of Economic Advisers. A symmetrical argument to the one above would ask whether their deliberations should not be illuminated with natural science knowledge. In so far as the CEA's principal concern extends increasingly beyond the short-run health of the economy into long-term economic development, it might well need technological experts quite as much as experts in economics (leaving aside the relation of psychology and sociology). The Commission, however, is not prepared to recommend, at the present time, the inclusion of non-economists in the Council's membership.

But we do urge the CEA to give explicit attention to the need for including in its professional staff and consultants: (1) persons drawn from the relevant social sciences outside economics, and (2) persons drawn from the natural sciences and engineering who can bring to bear relevant knowledge about scientific and technological trends and developments.

In summary, the Commission feels strongly that a policy of "integration" (emphatically *not* separate but equal treatment) should govern the relations of the social with the physical and biological sciences at top policy levels. We have given the positive reasons for our recommendations, but we need to mention also an implicit assumption on which it rests. The purpose of scientific advisory bodies is to give advice informed by scientific knowledge. If they come to include so many different types of experts that their deliberations have to become indistinguishable from the discussions of intelligent laymen, they have lost most of their special usefulness. For example, a PSAC composed of biologists who know no physics, *plus* social scientists who know no biology, *plus* physicists who know nothing of either biology or social science would be self-defeating.

Since we cannot confine public problems to fit within the boundaries of the disciplines, we must, therefore, seek to draw the membership of scientific advisory bodies from among those scientists who have some breadth of knowledge outside their personal research areas. Fortunately, a substantial number of social scientists have some professional background in the biological and physical sciences and mathematics; and some natural scientists have competence in one or more social science areas. We do not propose that "interdisciplinarianism" be made a condition of membership in federal science policy bodies. We *do* mean to suggest that, particularly in adding social science members, outstanding scientists be sought who are capable of translating and comprehending across the boundaries of the separate disciplines.

Effective Employment of Social Scientists in Government Agencies

At all levels of government, administrative agencies are perforce involved in applying the social sciences. Commerce, transportation, education, agriculture—all are parts of the complex social and economic structure of our society. Public health, social welfare, the courts, sanitation, and anti-pollution programs are also among the many areas of government responsibility in which the social sciences are relevant. And social scientists do, or should, participate in all phases of the many programs in cooperation with people from all other sciences and the professions. It is evident from recent events, for example, that engineering considerations alone are insufficient for planning transportation systems in metropolitan areas. Reemployment of the chronically unemployed is a complex social problem, and not simply a matter of finding jobs.

Governmental experience in social programs—such as the War on Poverty program—can help teach the important lesson that developing programs without careful social science consultation can be costly indeed. Staff who are well trained in the social sciences are essential resources in the development (and reformulation) of policies affecting our society. Social scientists properly belong at all staff levels and in all functions. Knowledge of the social sciences is needed in planning, research, development, implementation, monitoring, and evaluation.

Agency heads and top policy-making officials are not usually trained in one of the social sciences—nor need they be. Nevertheless, their definition of their agency's missions should incorporate recognition of the contributions that social science can offer. There is a commensurate responsibility upon social scientists to provide appropriately trained personnel.

In order to increase government use of the social sciences, programs must be developed that provide staff functions for social scientists, establish working environments that attract social scientists into government, enable government social scientists to keep abreast of changes in their disciplines, and develop relevant academic programs.

The professional in all sciences must be able to keep abreast of the literature and research of his technical field; and it is patently in the employer's interests to assure this. Federal government agencies—as well as those at other levels of government, and private employers—must extend the concept of continuing education to all professional employees and make formal provisions to implement the idea. Several steps are necessary in order to carry this out:

First, the universities and the federal agencies must develop jointly special academic programs to enable professional employees to bring themselves up-to-date with the very rapid developments of their own and related disciplines. University campuses are the obvious places for these courses because of the scholastic advantages of the academic environment.

Second, the federal government should institute an extensive, formal program of periodic leaves of one academic term at full salary (comparable to academic sabbatical leaves). Employees should have the choice of (1) taking the refresher curriculum mentioned above, (2) following their own course plans, (3) working upon a research project of their own choosing, or (4) planning a program that combines courses and research. Even research not directly related to their employment can contribute effectively to the currency of their knowledge. Because the federal government employs a large number of scientists throughout the country—only 10 per cent of all employees are based in Washington—it should consider multiple programs where its employees may take the refresher courses. Federal agencies have authority to carry out such programs under the Federal Government Training Act of 1958; and several agencies, such as the National Institute of Health, already have adopted such a program.

Providing Better Social Science Data

Regularly collected statistical data describing the state of major institutions and people in American society have been valuable in the development of successful policy formation and execution. The first national census of the United States, in 1790, was the forerunner of the current body of statistical information available to government administration, private corporations, labor unions, the American educational system, professional groups, and many others. Since the first United States census, and especially since the establishment of the Census Bureau, immensely valuable data have been produced by the federal government through its national surveys—and more recently through other offices such as the National Center for Health Statistics, the Department of Agriculture, the Bureau of Labor Statistics, the National Science Foundation, and so on.

Growing reliance on statistical data for policy decisions has led to an increased demand for data that can be used for projection and prediction. During the decade of the 1930's, the interest in "social indicators"—socially significant statistical descriptive data about American society, gathered in time series so as to show trends—was an important spur to the growth of the social sciences and a great step forward in their utilization. Over the years the social sciences have developed an ever greater capacity for measuring, evaluating, and predicting social change; at the same time the federal government has developed an increasing commitment to serve as a positive force in bringing about such change. Although there are still areas of uncertainty in the social sciences, although there are practical limits to the programs government can effectively manage, and although there are constitutional and political limits to the extension of federal authority, these two trends converge to produce a strong interest in the further development of statistical time-series data.

The same interest in social-indicator information is expressed at the municipality level, and of course by private industry. Data on labor relations, labor productivity, manpower resources, educational achievement, crime statistics, health and welfare data, consumer purchasing plans—to name but a few of the many significant indices—are proving increasingly valuable in the long-range planning and management of organizations.

The concept of social indicators is not new. More than twenty-five years ago Gunnar Myrdal admitted[3] that his group would have liked to present a general index, year by year, or at least decade by decade, of the status of the Negro in America; but he noted that the work of constructing and analyzing an index of Negro status in America amounted to a major investigation in itself and would have to be left for later research. In 1962, a report[4] of a panel established by the President's Science Advisory Committee recom-

---

[3] Gunnar Myrdal, *An American Dilemma* (New York: Harper & Row, 1944).
[4] Statement of Behavioral Sciences Subpanel of The Life Sciences Panel, President's Science Advisory Committee, *Strengthening the Behavioral Sciences* (Washington, D.C.: Government Printing Office, 1962).

mended that an effort be made by social science organizations to produce descriptive statistics on behavior in American society. Reports of three groups in 1965–1967[5] were concerned with data-storage centers and with the collection of social-indicator information. Interest is also evidenced in the directive from the President to the Department of Health, Education, and Welfare to make a report to him on the social state of the nation—resulting in the recently issued *Toward a Social Report*,[6] which covers perhaps a half-dozen aspects of American social life. At the same time the academic world has been active, producing the volume edited by Raymond A. Bauer entitled *Social Indicators*[7] and the recently published *Indicators of Social Change*.[8]

What practical steps can be taken now to provide better information about the state of the nation? The Commission's recommendations are threefold:

1. *Increasing the range of social indicators*. The first major task is to expand the current national effort in collecting statistical time-series data. Even though substantial information is now being collected, many important areas of American life proceed either without record, or with inadequate or too-infrequent statistical description. Planned social improvement can hardly be optimally effective when the planners have no information on either social trends, or the probable consequences of a new federal social policy.

Not only should the present United States decennial census be strongly supported and expanded in its coverage, but consideration should be given to more frequent national surveys (quarterly, or even monthly) and to an increase in federally sponsored, special

---

[5] Committee on Preservation and Use of Economic Data, "Report of the Committee . . . to the Social Science Research Council, April 1965," in *The Computer and Invasion of Privacy: Hearings Before a Subcommittee of the Committee on Government Operations, House of Representatives, 89th Congress, 2nd Session, July 26, 27, and 28, 1966, Appendix 1* (Washington, D.C.: Government Printing Office, 1966), 195–253.

E. S. Dunn, Jr., *Review of Proposal for a National Data Center*, Statistical Evaluation Report No. 6 (Washington, D.C.: Executive Office of the President, Bureau of the Budget, Office of Statistical Standards, December, 1965). (Reprinted in United States House of Representatives, Committee on Government Operations, Subcommittee on Invasion of Privacy, *The Computer and Invasion of Privacy: Hearings Before the Subcommittee*. [Washington, D.C.: Government Printing Office, 1966], 254–294.)

C. Kaysen, *Report of the Task Force on the Storage of and Access to Government Statistics* (Washington, D.C.: Executive Office of the President, Bureau of the Budget, October, 1966). (Reprinted in United States Senate, Committee on the Judiciary, Subcommittee on Administrative Practice and Procedure, *Computer Privacy: Hearings Before the Subcommittee* [Washington, D.C.: Government Printing Office, 1967], 25–37.)

[6] U.S. Department of Health, Education, and Welfare, *Toward a Social Report* (Washington, D.C.: Government Printing Office, 1969).

[7] Raymond A. Bauer, *Social Indicators* (Cambridge, Mass.: Massachusetts Institute of Technology Press, 1966).

[8] Eleanor Bernert Sheldon and Wilbert E. Moore, *Indicators of Social Change* (New York: Russell Sage Foundation, 1968). See also: Bertram M. Gross, "Social Goals and Indicators for American Society," Vols. I and II, *THE ANNALS* of The American Academy of Political and Social Science, Philadelphia (May and September, 1967).

small-area statistical censuses. The costs of such increased social-data collection are so great that the government is the only institution that can possibly bear the burden. Substantial new government funds must be earmarked for this important task.

Nongovernment, university-affiliated research centers can, however, assume partial responsibility for fact-gathering under public support. Survey research centers, in particular, can identify gaps in available statistical information and carry out some of the needed research. Under private support, moreover, nongovernment research centers can collect data where the desirable social statistics may be politically sensitive. It is also for the nongovernmental groups to work on the creation of new statistical series and topics which in their experimental stage may be too esoteric to be justified as a public expense, but which may provide the basis for future federal collection of data when their value has been demonstrated. Private research groups, finally, can make valuable critical evaluations of methods used in producing social indicators, and can develop new and experimental sampling research procedures. Substantial federal support, by the National Science Foundation in particular, should be used to stimulate the development of new social indicators by survey research centers and related institutions.

2. *Providing data linkages.* In this section, and in the one that immediately follows, the Commission presents its recommendations on the establishment of statistical data centers, and the related problem of protection of privacy. The Commission is deeply concerned about protecting privacy, and such statistical data centers should not be allowed, indeed, unless safeguards to individual and institutional privacy can be guaranteed. "Data linkage" can be defined as the bringing together of information collected by different organizations about different sectors of society, so that data relationships can be studied and reported. For example, improving the performance of both the economy and the rest of society requires a complex working knowledge of how the economy operates, how society changes, and how the economy and society interact with each other. To illustrate specifically: We need to know not only whether changes in the discount rate will require tax-rate changes, but more importantly we need to know the employment consequences of such intervention. And we should know not only the consequences for the labor market in general, but also for different occupations and industries; for the skilled and unskilled; white and nonwhite; teenagers and elderly.

Statistical data obtained by federal agencies for both general and administrative purposes currently provide the basis for examining the social and economic factors affecting the nation. Over twenty separate bureaus are engaged in the collection and compilation of these data. With such dispersion of collection and processing, pooled use of federal statistical resources is difficult; but federal agencies are beginning to express interest in establishing such data linkages. The Urban Information Systems Interagency Committee, for instance, is interested in developing, at the local level (county, regional, etc.), information systems and subsystems.

While both the theoretical and the data bases for exemplary data linkages need further development, there has been progress. Efforts at small-scale data linkage, both within and among federal agencies, have already demonstrated the value of this work. For instance, Social Security Administration administrative records are valuable for providing information that is longitudinally linked:

(a) Cumulative and linked information obtained from the hospital insurance program, on episodes of hospitalization and the utilization of medical services, provides a basic resource for studying health conditions of the aged.

(b) Dynamics of labor supply, labor mobility between industries, and different locations and patterns of lifetime earnings, can be investigated through longitudinal record linkages of administrative data at the Social Security Administration. Certainly, such studies have bearing on the interaction between economic policy and labor supply and composition.

To illustrate further, the general-purpose statistics of the Bureau of the Census can be linked with those from the administrative records of the Internal Revenue Service, the Social Security Administration, and with vital statistics—to provide reliability estimates of the basic data and to improve the quality of these data, as well as to provide "new" information.

(a) Updated population estimates and tracings of migration patterns for small areas may be possible through such data-linkage studies. Such materials are particularly useful to municipalities and local planning boards in the allocating of resources.

(b) Information on the social and economic factors affecting variations in births, deaths, and causes of death is clearly valuable for public-health policies; and can be made accessible through record linkages matching vital statistics and census returns.

(c) Data linkage techniques can be employed in program evaluation follow-up. For example, the effect of the Job Corps or other similar programs may be assessed, in part, by relating

Social Security Administration longitudinal earning records to the demographic variables of those exposed to these programs. Through record linkages, experimental and control cohorts may also be compared.

Efforts to develop data linkages must take into account at least two concerns of social scientists.

First, no attempt should be made to imitate an aggregate like the gross national product. If we made the mistake of producing some overall composite index of the nation's social health, it would have to be an amalgam of different and quite disparate measures, and as such probably meaningless. We need data linkages of a simple order, as described above.

Second, there is a controversy among protagonists of social indicators about the relative emphasis to be placed on the current "problem definition" value of indicators versus their theoretical quality. There is, on the one hand, a demand for indicators closely related to social problems or policy concerns, local or national— the degree of interracial prejudice; the distribution of white and nonwhite children in school classrooms; the number of diagnosed alcoholics among men of a given age; or the crime rate by population density and urban area.

On the other hand, social scientists call attention to the danger that social statistics intended as aids to policy formation, although admittedly valuable, may become controlling factors. Policy-makers often find themselves constrained (by economy or partisanship) to use only data gathered for operational purposes. But such data, so the opposing argument goes, presuppose the very organizational framework and problem definitions under review—and effectively close off the possibility of new points of view and new attacks upon the problems. The proponents of this view are more concerned with the analysis of significant trends in American society than with short-term solutions; they plead for the development of indicators that, while not so immediately applicable to policy formation, seem to offer a better understanding of the forces producing change in American society over the long run.

An important attempt[9] to conceptualize the latter problem proposes four major divisions for examining structural changes in American society and its constituent features: (1) the demographic base, giving an indication of aggregative population trends, and the changing composition and distribution of populations across the nation's surface; (2) major structural components of the society, examining the functionally distinct ways in which a

---

[9] Sheldon and Moore, *op. cit.*

society produces goods, organizes its knowledge and technology, reproduces itself, and maintains order; (3) distributive features of the society, looking at how the products of society—people, goods, services, knowledge, values, and order—get allocated across the several sectors of the American population; (4) aggregative features of the society, suggesting how the system as a whole changes with respect to its inequalities and varying opportunities and in terms of its social welfare.

The Commission views the conflict between these two points of view as a mutually healthy and productive challenge.

3. *Protecting privacy.* The recommendation that data linkages be made between selected federal government statistics raises the disquieting and most important question of how the individual right to privacy is to be protected.

In Luther J. Carter's discussion of this problem he says:

The computer, for all its promise and achievements as a tool of modern technology, is viewed with distrust by many people who have considered its implications for personal privacy. They are uneasy at the possibility that someday, perhaps well before 1984, there will exist a master computer center, a Big Brother, with voluminous and instantly retrievable data on every American who has lived long enough to get a social security number, a traffic ticket, or even a birth certificate, or a report card from school. The fact that private credit-rating bureaus and insurance investigators already have dossiers on tens of millions of Americans itself gives substance to these fears and is beginning to receive attention from Congress. However, insofar as the computer and personal privacy is concerned, the question which has received the most congressional attention to date is that of whether the United States government should establish a statistical data center or "national data bank."

Such a data center—first proposed in 1965 by a committee of the Social Science Research Council, a nongovernmental group, and later endorsed by a government task force—would be intended to serve, not investigators seeking information about individual persons, but, rather, scholars and other users of gross statistics. One of its principal aims would be to help economists, other social scientists, and government specialists investigate major economic and social problems, such as those of persistent unemployment and social disorganization in the big-city slums.

A score of federal agencies, such as the Census Bureau, the Internal Revenue Service, and the Social Security Administration, collect data of various kinds. The national data center would store the more statistically significant data collected by these agencies, and, as required for special studies, data from two or more agencies would be matched up and integrated. In a study of the causes of poverty, for example, it might be useful to have census data integrated with data obtained from the social security and internal revenue systems. Most social scientists who use federal statistics extensively probably support the data-bank concept, though there now appears to be a general belief that special efforts must be made to safeguard privacy.[10]

Protection of privacy must come through many and widely varying channels. Computer manufacturers, software firms, time-sharing agencies, professional associations, user groups, social scientists, legislative committees, administrative agencies—all these groups must be involved. The manufacturers of computers and the so-called software (computer program) producers must plan computer designs and operations to provide greater safeguards in data-storage and retrieval systems. Computer operators must add to their professional responsibilities the protection of access to data-storage systems. At the same time, legislation on what persons have access to what information about organizations or individuals needs further development. Finally, identification checks of all users of such systems should be established to provide records that can be followed up in case of suspected abuse.

Currently several national organizations, public and private, are engaged in planning major studies of privacy and due process issues in computer data banks, and these will provide much desired leadership in work on the problem of privacy. At the same time the Bureau of the Budget is actively seeking the development of necessary regulations to guide access to federal statistical information. These efforts should be strongly supported because they promise to produce the combination of safeguards that will assure privacy and still allow the development of data-linkage systems.

To summarize the Commission's views on better data collection, we recommend the following: First, the federal government, universities, and private funding groups should provide the resources necessary for both government and small research organizations to develop new, more frequent, and better social statistics to record the important aspects of American life as yet relatively unstudied. Second, the government should provide for increased linkages between the bodies of data now routinely collected. But, third, this must go hand in hand with both federal and private efforts to develop the means for protection of privacy, and data linkages should not be made unless individual and institutional privacy can be protected.

[10] Luther J. Carter, "National Data Bank: Its Advocates Try to Erase 'Big Brother' Image," *Science*, 163 (January 20, 1969), 160–162. See also Alan Westin, *Privacy and Freedom* (New York: Atheneum Press, 1967), and Jack Sawyer and Howard Schechter, "Computers, Privacy, and the National Data Center," *American Psychologist* (November, 1968), 810–818.

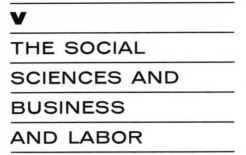

V

THE SOCIAL
SCIENCES AND
BUSINESS
AND LABOR

Business

Although the relations between parts of the social science community and parts of the community of business leadership have been less than friendly, the occasional public acrimony may have concealed a good deal of interdependence. One may of course still encounter the business executive who rests his wisdom on accumulated experience rather than the application of abstract principles. And one may encounter social scientists who regard any interest in the organization and functioning of business firms as a fraternizing with the enemy. Such mutual suspicion is increasingly rare, as the complexities of knowledge requisite to sensible decision are recognized by executives, and as the "living laboratories" of human behavior in large organizations (such as business corporations) provide opportunities for social scientists to observe and analyze.

Illustrations of social science contributions to business activities are the use of statisticians as well as economists in forecasting business conditions and the effects on the individual company, and in planning, scheduling production, and steadying employment; the assistance of social scientists in attempting to determine consumer needs and demands and best methods of communication; the role of industrial relations executives, with the assistance of actuaries, economists, lawyers, and sociologists in developing employee benefit plans—pensions, health insurance, life insurance, disability insurance, and the like—to protect individuals against economic hazards. (The cost of such plans is now about 25 per cent of the payroll of the average company.) Other examples follow in more detail.

Some past attempts to introduce systematic principles into personnel selection and work organization came from the hands of engineers. Frederick W. Taylor's espousal of "scientific management" late in the nineteenth century had only modest success, mainly because of erroneous assumptions about human motivation. Later attempts, such as those sponsored by the Research Division of the Harvard Graduate School of Business Administration in the interwar years, sought to rectify earlier assumptions and policies by emphasizing "human relations in industry." This again led to some distortions, however, as it exaggerated the nonrational conduct of workers (though presumably not of managers). Yet, studies of informal work groups and informal channels of communication within formally constituted organizations have had an enduring effect on the perception of how complex industrial systems really operate.

One of the earlier, and continuing, applications of social science in business has been the use of aptitude and personality tests in personnel selection and placement. Later, as technical change often proceeded independently of consideration of human attributes, more attention came to be given to the design of machines with men (their operators) in mind. The industrial engineer and the industrial psychologist had to make common cause.

The complexities of corporate dealings with organized labor and with administrative agencies of the government led initially and naturally to an increased demand for legal services. Yet, the problems, and the expert knowledge necessary for solution or compromise, were not entirely legal in character. Employee morale came to be recognized as not assured simply by "fair dealing" in collective bargaining with labor unions. The significance of size and diversification for the structure of market competition called for expert advice from economists. The introduction of new products, although still subject to considerable uncertainty and error, may be approached with somewhat greater confidence if preceded by market analysis involving sample surveys and related observational techniques from the social sciences.

Until fairly recently the training of the business executive (or union leader) did not alert him to the uses of social science. Even if the executive had graduate study in business administration, the practically exclusive reliance on the analysis and discussion of "cases" in business decisions was almost anti-intellectual in character. The underlying common principles were minimized, and the importance of securing and assessing expert knowledge relevant to decisions was mostly neglected. Now, however, contemporary graduate business school curricula and business managements have widely imported and absorbed the techniques of decision theory, simulation models, modern statistical methods, and other products of social science research.

Currently, many university and other research agency resources are devoted to the problems of business administration and to the training of managements in social science knowledge as applied to business decisions. Moreover, a very considerable use of public money has been involved in the education of business executives. Business school faculties, particularly, have done research in enterprises that has carried over to consultant positions. At the same time "management development programs," calculated to assure a pool of executive talent skilled in the applications of social science findings, have blossomed both in corporations and universities, and special programs in modern business techniques have been developed for the training of mid-career executives, by business schools and by business associations such as the American Management Association, working through conferences, seminars, and discussion groups. Thus, specialized institutions have emerged to disseminate social science advances to large-scale enterprises and to provide a conduit between social science research and the mainstream of business executives.

Corporations have also recruited social research in such sensitive areas as the introduction and management of change and have thereby reduced many of the tensions generated in modern industrial life. The lessons from this research have, simultaneously, facilitated the development of programs increasingly undertaken by corporations with respect to the so-called hardcore unemployed.

In an age of "multinational" corporations, it is hardly surprising that corporate leaders also find useful the findings and counsel of anthropologists, historians, and others who have special skills in the analysis of different cultures—whether for marketing or other purposes. The delicate relations between American guests and foreign hosts is no less problematical than the more strictly economic efforts of the executives overseas in an age of heightened local sensitivities, rapid change, and nationalistic impulses.

Much needs to be done, and can be done, to further facilitate a constructive, and scientifically productive, exchange between the corporate and social science communities. Thus, there is a need for more trained personnel to staff the social science departments in the nation's university schools of business. Many of these schools have recently shown themselves to be among the most exciting centers on American campuses. Indeed, these schools may take significant credit for pushing hard to train business executives with a very broad view of their responsibilities in a democratic society, as well as with a consciously scientific attitude toward their work as managers.

The discussion so far has focused on examples of the utilization of social science in the current conduct of business. Some of these examples represent the application of general principles to the particular problems in business policies and procedures, or the transfer of "practical" knowledge—say, theories of organization and "operations research" or other rational decision models—from one setting to another. Sooner or later, however, knowledge relevant to business must rest in considerable part on actual studies of business organization and its rapidly changing social setting. Here, too, the recent and current situation is uneven. For example, some students of the "economics of the firm" do not limit their analyses to how an ideal firm "ought" to act under stipulated conditions, but study the comparative behavior of actual firms. Yet much work of this latter sort remains to be done, and the task is not made easier by diversified firms and conglomerates that compete in a multitude of very different markets.

Similarly, numerous sociological studies have reconfirmed the existence and importance of informal groups at the workplace, but few comparable studies of informal managerial groups and procedures exist. "Office politics" is more the subject of rumor, the plot for a novel, or the folklore of the suburban cocktail set, than the subject of sober inquiry. Few political scientists have studied the corporation as a private state, complete with legislative and executive functions, and perhaps needful of a judiciary.

A principal problem for the researcher, of course, is access to information. The business firm is a private organization. Except for the information made public to stockholders (and others) by corporations listed on a regular stock exchange, the corporation has the same claims to privacy and confidentiality as the individual. Moreover, cooperation in research has hidden costs, even when one does not fear revelation of privileged information to a competitor—if for no other reason than the nuisance of interrupting busy schedules to supply information.

Problems of financial support for research occur in this field as in others. It might seem odd that research on the corporation, a principal source of wealth-production in the economy, should lack support. Yet, the corporation is organized as a profit-seeking organization, and may properly decline to support abstract "fundamental," or even long-range, studies. Research of general relevance to the business community may be too remote to justify support by individual companies.

Both public and private support for social science research relevant to business has been understandably most generous for studies in economics. The Departments of Commerce and Labor, the Federal Reserve Board, the Council of Economic Advisers, the regulatory commissions, and a large variety of other agencies have research staffs in economics; and some support research by university-based economists. The largest foundation program, the Ford Foundation's support for "economic development and business administration," has also favored economic research, though not exclusively.

The changing position of the business or industrial corporation in the troubled urban community; the still indefinite limits of what constitutes the "social responsibility" of the corporation; the much-debated effects of large organizations on the lives of their inhabitants—these are some of the problems that the Commission notes as being on the continuing agenda for sound, and often critical, research bearing on the way business now operates and might operate in the future.

Labor Organizations and Collective Bargaining

William Sylvis and the National Labor Union, just a century ago, advocated the creation of a Department of Labor and the gathering of labor statistics. Resolutions at these union conventions also sought detailed industrial data in the Census of 1870. One complained that,

> It is easier to tell how many horses are well stabled than how many families are well housed—easy to find out all that concern the capitalist, but difficult to discover the actual condition of the great mass of the people. . . .[1]

The first Bureau of Labor Statistics was established in Massachusetts in 1869, and Carrol D. Wright became first commissioner of the federal bureau in 1885.[2]

Today there are very substantial collections of descriptive materials and statistical data gathered by governmental sources, private groups, and by labor and management organizations themselves. Social scientists have made extensive studies of the labor market, the workplace, and collective bargaining. The present utilization of the social sciences, and the opportunities for more imaginative collaboration, are separately considered below for labor organiza-

---

[1] John Lombardi, *Labor's Voice in the Cabinet* (New York: Columbia University Press, 1942), 24; also Jonathan Grossman, *William Sylvis, Pioneer of American Labor* (New York: Columbia University Press, 1945), 255–256.
[2] James Leiby, *Carrol Wright and Labor Reform, The Origin of Labor Statistics* (Cambridge, Mass.: Harvard University Press, 1960).

tions in their internal decision-making and for the parties engaged in collective bargaining.

Internal union operations. Most of the studies of internal union affairs have been made in the United States by labor economists and labor historians; more recently a number have been the work of sociologists, and occasionally a political scientist has turned his attention to labor organizations. As labor unions have hired professional staff, such as economists, social science literature has become known to those working in labor unions. The Industrial Relations Research Association and the National Academy of Arbitrators, and a number of specialized professional journals such as the *Industrial and Labor Relations Review,* have helped to provide more interchange between scholars and practitioners and to diffuse the results of research.

Only rarely, however, have social science techniques been used by labor organizations in their own internal decision-making processes. In a few instances survey research methods have been used to gather the preferences of union members in preparation for negotiations, to appraise shifting views of members on political and community issues,[3] to seek judgments of members on the policies and leadership of the organization, and to survey members for purposes of national election campaigns.[4]

In labor organizations there are no well-developed means for the transmission and diffusion of new social science knowledge and for its direct application and interplay with practical applications.[5] There are numerous opportunities, nonetheless, for the fruitful and systematic application of modern organization theory and other social science knowledge to the problems that confront labor leaders—both in the formulation of internal policy and the administration of these complex organizations. The techniques of modern organizational planning, budgeting, and personnel development, which have grown out of social science research and have been so widely applied in large-scale enterprises, can be adapted to unions.

Social science knowledge can make a significant contribution to

[3] *Report on Union Member Attitude Survey, Conducted Among Locals in the Central Labor Council of Alameda County,* Institute of Industrial Relations (Berkeley: University of California, 1964).

[4] Alexander E. Barkan, "The Union Member: Profile and Attitude," *The American Federationist,* 74 (August, 1967), 1–5.

[5] Union officers come from the ranks and have had appreciably lower levels of education than business executives, although educational levels of union officers are rising with those of the population. A recent study showed that 21 per cent of national union officers had completed a college education compared to 57 per cent of business executives. (Abraham Friedman, "Characteristics of National and International Union Leaders" [unpublished ms., Graduate School of Business, University of Chicago, October, 1967].)

a number of difficult questions that confront major international unions.[6] There is need to appraise organizing methods and procedures, particularly with the youth and with occupations not traditionally well-organized. The problems of gaining the attachment of women employees and preserving the interest and loyalty of members moving from the inner city to the suburbs deserve particular attention. The appropriate size of local unions and the relationship of dues structure to the quality of service to members is a vital question. The perplexing problem of the role unions should seek in the community in dealing with urban problems involves the interests and preferences of members and an appraisal as to the tractability of various approaches to these problems. What role, if any, should a union seek in the administration of a health clinic, in an urban manpower training program, or in the allocation of pension fund resources to the social purposes of low-cost housing?

The most direct and continuous relationship between academic social science and the trade union movement has been through various Institutes of Industrial and Labor Relations at state universities such as Berkeley, Los Angeles, Wisconsin, Cornell, Rutgers, and several other states. For the most part, these efforts have been principally in labor education, though the research studies in these institutes have been a source of knowledge both for trade unions and management. This research has largely been on economic issues, though on occasion they have included sociological and psychological surveys, including studies of membership attitudes. In recent years, the increased participation of trade unions in prepaid medical plans (e.g., Blue Cross–Blue Shield) has led the unions to a greater interest in the operations of such health systems and the measures of their efficiency, and such interest has prompted scholarly studies in institutes on these questions.

The major problem in the application of social science knowledge to these internal problems of labor organizations is the absence of any mechanism for continuing contact between academic research and a capability within the labor movement to develop applications. The emergence of a research group at the AFL-CIO level with time for more basic questions, rather than with immediate operational responsibilities, is necessary if the labor movement is to become more responsive. The Federation level could well provide the basis for cooperation with constituent national unions and for the dissemination of the results of research and experiments.

The social advantages of applying social science knowledge to

---

[6] In 1966, 20 out of 190 international unions had more than 250,000 members. These unions included almost two-thirds of all union members.

internal problems confronting unions would well warrant foundation support for such an institutional development.[7] There is increasing recognition within the Federation of the need for and potentials of such a mechanism.

Collective bargaining. The social sciences have contributed to the process of collective bargaining, including arbitration, by providing a large and growing volume of general information about the economic environment and other features of the social system within which negotiations arise. A variety of statistical series—those relating to unemployment, cost-of-living, wage changes, profits and production, for example—provide a context for the negotiations. The parties, and their experts, are familiar with these data and argue their view of the outlook and the merits of their proposals for settlement in terms of such measurements. Such data do not uniquely specify a settlement, but the discourse and argument is often couched in terms of these environmental features. Moreover, putting the argument in these terms tends to facilitate the mutual understanding of the other's perspective, and provides a rationalization for changing positions which is essential to agreement-making. The perfection of information on the economic climate and greater confidence in specifying the outlook may be expected to make a further contribution to the resolution of disputes.

The detailed study by particular parties of difficult problems—pensions and retirement, efficiency and stabilization of employment, manpower planning, adjustment to technological change, and the like—provides a significant opportunity to apply social science knowledge and techniques. Such study groups have been initiated by the parties or by the government when confronted with the prospect of continuing conflict.[8]

The adjustment of work rules in the collective bargaining agreement covering West Coast longshoremen in 1960 was preceded by a detailed study of employment patterns and age distributions; the systematic review of government procurement policies was significant to the reduction of disputes on missile and space sites in the early 1960's; the study of the quality of medical care under health and welfare plans has had major consequences on the provision of medical care in some communities. Such special projects

---

[7] As a parallel, consider the role of the Committee for Economic Development, which has provided a means for interaction between business opinion and academic specialists in a research setting.

[8] William Gomberg, "Special Study Committees," in John T. Dunlop and Neil W. Chamberlain (eds.), *Frontiers of Collective Bargaining* (New York: Harper & Row, 1967), 235–251.

provide the opportunity for the most intensive use of social science research results. The procedures could be improved to mobilize social science experts in such studies in the Labor Department and the Federal Mediation and Conciliation Service.

An examination of the frontiers of collective bargaining suggests that new opportunities are also emerging for the application of social science research. The parties to collective bargaining are likely to be increasingly concerned in tight labor markets with training and education for the workplace; with the productive employment of the disadvantaged (including minority groups); with providing a greater measure of self-determination to higher education employees; and with the redesigning of jobs and supervision to meet these new expectations. On these questions, social science research has both something to contribute and something to learn.

VI

THE SOCIAL
SCIENCES AND
COMMUNITY
ORGANIZATIONS

A significant portion of the nation's social problems are attacked by various community organizations in small towns, medium-sized cities, and metropolitan areas. Many of these organizations are concerned with public health and medical care, education, welfare, mental health, intergroup relations, child development, and so on. The term "community organizations" includes both public and private agencies that deliver services or solve problems at the community level. These include departments of local government, such as the police, fire, health and welfare departments; and voluntary charitable organizations, such as family service groups, settlement houses, child welfare organizations, socially active fraternal organizations, and many others.

The Commission views the contributions of the social sciences to the effective operation of community organizations as an opportunity for immediate, and direct, utilization of the social sciences in on-site social-action programs. Information about the contributions of social scientists to community organizations is at present very diffuse, and much more may be taking place than is immediately evident in any informal appraisal.

By way of introductory illustration, one highly successful interaction between social scientists and community organizations dates from 1915, when a Bureau of Municipal Research was established in the City of Rochester, New York. It is staffed by professional social scientists and its purpose is to evaluate and improve local government in Rochester and surrounding areas, through nonpartisan research. The Bureau has carried out numerous studies in the areas of urban socioeconomic problems, municipal management

73

and reforms, fiscal management, justice and rehabilitation, research tools and methods, education and culture, and state legislation.

Another, more recent and consequently perhaps more familiar, illustration is the current employment by New York City of the RAND Corporation to make certain policy studies. RAND–New York is probably the largest (about forty full-time professionals) policy research effort in the United States devoted to urban problems; it is considering research in such areas as fire prevention, police operations, and the city's housing and health programs. It is interdisciplinary—including mathematicians, computer experts, engineers,' operations research specialists, social scientists, and physicians. The staff has close daily contacts with officials of the City of New York and with employees in the Mayor's Office, the Budget Bureau, and in the relevant City Departments.

Social scientists have been influential in getting the St. Louis Board of Police Commissioners to change its conception of the chronic public-drunkenness offender from being a criminal to being medically ill. Other illustrations include the work of social scientists in the St. Louis County Health Department; and with the State Charities Aid Association in New York City, the Child Welfare League, the Jewish Family Service Association, again in New York City.

Another example is the work of social scientists in settlement-house programs, particularly the research of David Caplovitz in New York City on installment-credit practices among the poor. His work gave a substantial impetus to the concern with installment-credit practices at both state and federal levels, and to the formation of consumers' protective associations.

Municipal planning and development agencies; police departments; health, welfare, and recreation agencies; schools and colleges—all these have their own specific functions and problems. Yet there are areas of social science knowledge relevant to all or most of them. Some of these areas are discussed below.

There is, at the disposal of administrators of both governmental and nongovernmental agencies, a social science theory and also empirical findings on the structure and functioning of organizations. A body of knowledge is thus available on such issues as the process of organizational change; the relation of internal communication patterns to efficiency in organizations; organizational rigidity and innovativeness; and the effects of different leadership styles. Of specific interest to administrators are studies of differential participation among voluntary associations, and the role played by voluntary associations in influencing public policy.[1] Other studies have indicated that there is differential access to community organizations, and differential treatment of persons according to their social status, by such organizations. Examples include medical diagnosis and treatment; arrests and court dispositions for juvenile delinquency and adult crime; and treatment by professional practitioners such as guidance counselors, social workers, and so on through a long list.[2]

One hypothesis for differential treatment by social status is that members of the groups getting poorer treatment are not represented in determining the policies of community organizations, and therefore cannot insist upon equal treatment for their groups. One group of studies involves attempts to bring about community change or to develop community programs through a coalition strategy such as that used by community organization workers and community development workers.[3] A related group of studies investigates various types of resistance by residents to an agent of change who comes in from the outside or who represents a different social class or subculture.[4]

In recent years more sophisticated efforts have been made to understand the specific ways in which community organizations fit in with the institutional patterns of American living. Officially, they are designed to accomplish identifiable (though often vague) objectives. Actually, it has been found that, in numerous instances, they do not address the problems that they are supposed to; they do not reach the appropriate population groups; often, whether deliberately or inadvertently, they perform entirely different functions from those they were intended to perform. A familiar example is the public welfare system, which is intended to support needy families and individuals through income maintenance and to help them to become as self-sufficient as possible. Certain studies have shown that the public welfare system stultifies efforts at self-sufficiency, reduces self-confidence rather than enhances it, and performs various functions that restrict the behavior of the

---

[1] For example, see William A. Glaser and D. L. Sills (eds.), *Government of Associations* (Totowa, N.J.: Bedminster Press, Inc., 1966), and Charles R. Wright and Herbert H. Hyman, "Voluntary Association Memberships of American Adults: Evidence from National Sample Surveys," *American Sociological Review*, 23 (1958), 284–294.

[2] An excellent study in this area is August B. Hollingshead and Frederick C. Redlich, *Social Class and Mental Illness: A Community Study* (New York: John Wiley & Sons, Inc., 1958).

[3] See, for example, Murray G. Ross, *Case Histories in Community Organizations* (New York: Harper & Row, 1958), and Christopher Sower *et al.*, *Community Involvement: The Webs of Formal and Informal Ties That Make for Action* (New York: Free Press, 1957).

[4] See, for example, Benjamin D. Paul (ed.), *Health, Culture, and Community* (New York: Russell Sage Foundation, 1955), and Edward H. Spicer, *Human Problems in Technological Change* (New York: Russell Sage Foundation, 1952).

recipients rather than provide additional life alternatives.[5] Further research is needed to discover why some public welfare programs have these unwanted effects.

Many community organizations attempt to change the attitudes, behavior, or living conditions of target populations. Large expenditures of resources are involved in such efforts, yet adequate evaluation of achievements has rarely taken place. Further, when carefully-designed research studies have been carried out, they have often shown the programs have been only minimally effective.[6]

On the basis of evidence of many diverse examples of social science use in community organizations, and of the existence of certain bodies of social science knowledge that seem useful in improving the operations of community-level organizations, the Commission believes that opportunities for this kind of direct practical social science application should be much more completely appraised. A needed first step is a comprehensive inventory (on a national basis) of the social science work going on in community organizations. This should identify the notable successes, in order to isolate the common elements in such successful collaboration. Identification of successful programs, however, is not possible until better evaluative research studies are carried out to determine the degree to which community organizations have been able to achieve their goals. The Commission recommends, therefore, that many more careful evaluation efforts be carried out by experts who are well-informed about the local scene.

Second, a systematic appraisal should be made of the opportunities for social science to be brought to bear in community organizations. Some elements of this overall appraisal now exist in separate studies (e.g., in regard to the police, and to community mental health services), but these have not been brought together and reviewed from the comprehensive perspective of the possible contributions of the social sciences at the community level. The Commission therefore recommends that such a systematic national appraisal be undertaken, either by an appropriate government organization or through a task force or commission sponsored from the private sector. Without such an appraisal, there can be no basis for sounder planning to further develop collaboration between the social sciences and community organizations.

Since successful demonstrations of social science contributions

---

[5] See, for example, Elaine Cumming, *Systems of Social Regulation* (New York: Atherton Press, 1968).
[6] See, for example, Henry J. Meyer, Edgar F. Borgatta, and Wyatt C. Jones, *Girls at Vocational High* (New York: Russell Sage Foundation, 1965), and Edwin Powers and Helen Witmer, *An Experiment in the Prevention of Juvenile Delinquency: The Cambridge-Somerville Youth Study* (New York: Columbia University Press, 1951).

already exist in some number, the Commission wishes, at the same time, to encourage the support of existing channels for the dissemination of such knowledge. Most typically, the transfer of useful information takes place through social scientists in various relationships to community organizations—consulting, for example —and through the employment of social scientists in a staff or research capacity for a short- or long-term period. Information is also transferred through workshops, institutes, and conferences between organization representatives and social scientists. Yet a third channel is provided by special journals dealing with community organizations (such as *Social Issues, Community Mental Health,* and the *Journal of Health and Social Behavior,* to name just a few) which are important vehicles for the diffusion of new social science knowledge.

After our above recommendations concerning social scientists and community organizations have been carried out, we think it desirable in the long run that there should be available to such organizations—perhaps through some federal agency—the opportunity to have an assessment made of how they might benefit from social science knowledge and techniques. Funds should then be made available to the community organizations themselves in order to implement well-planned requests. We believe that community organizations, both public and private, are definite frontiers of possible social science utilization and, as such, deserve systematic exploration.

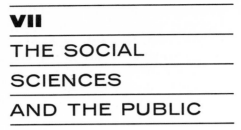

VII

THE SOCIAL

SCIENCES

AND THE PUBLIC

Improved dissemination of social science knowledge to the public is important for two reasons. First, the knowledge and insights of the social sciences are directly applicable by the individual to his own life—particularly in such areas as career planning, childrearing, and voluntary community activities. Second, a more receptive attitude and increased knowledge among the general public will raise the public expectations as to the value of social science in dealing with public problems.

Most social science education occurs in college, and in graduate and professional schools. Nevertheless, there are still great opportunities to advance the teaching of social sciences in the elementary and secondary schools; and at the other end of the spectrum, the Commission believes that continuing education for adults provides another frontier in the transmission of social science knowledge and its utilization.

Social Science Education in Elementary and Secondary Schools

Teaching the social science curriculum in secondary schools and, to a lesser extent, in elementary schools is a major enterprise of American education; it is potentially a powerful force for the transmission of social science knowledge to the public. The concern of the Commission has been with curriculum improvement; we note the need to improve the training and qualifications for teaching the social sciences, but are not addressing ourselves to this problem here.

1. *Content of the curriculum.* The social science curriculum is the concern of many organizations and special groups, and specific

efforts to improve the social science curriculum—too numerous to list here—are in progress in the United States.[1] The National Council for the Social Studies is the primary professional organization of social science and social studies teachers. This organization, through its meetings, committees, and publications,[2] is concerned with curriculum. But it has had difficulty in wielding a strong influence for change (1) because of the heterogeneity of the American educational system, and (2) because its liaison with the professional social science associations has not been effective in all areas.

The Commission views as especially important recent efforts by professional social scientists themselves to work on the social science curriculum for elementary and secondary schools. Many distinguished social scientists of the past generation and longer have given time to this endeavor, and their work has been valuable. In very recent years, a most significant development has been the concern of the national professional social science associations to make an organized effort to develop sound, up-to-date materials for elementary and secondary school teaching. In these organized efforts, anthropology and economics are the farthest along. Geography and sociology started their efforts a few years ago; and psychology and political science have not yet organized to meet this need.[3] In the areas other than economics, which is funded separately through the Joint Council on Economic Education, the National Science Foundation has provided desirable leadership and support.

For illustration, a more specific report on the efforts in sociology describes progress as follows: Sociological Resources for Social Studies, under the auspices of the American Sociological Association, was funded by the National Science Foundation beginning in August, 1964. It is producing three kinds of materials for high schools. The first of these is a set of some thirty-five short units called "episodes," suitable for existing senior high school social science and social studies courses. The idea behind these short units is: Since there is unlikely to be a great increase in the number of sociology courses taught in high schools in the near future, the most effective line of action is to familiarize students with the perspectives and generalizations of sociology by utilizing existing courses. Episodes cover a wide range of topics, from poverty and

---

[1] The U.S. Office of Education is a major supporter of these projects. See "A Directory of Social Studies Projects," *Social Education*, XXXI (October, 1967).
[2] E.g., *Social Education*, the official journal of the organization, and yearbooks, bulletins, curriculum series, etc.
[3] The Commission on the Humanities in the Schools (supported by the National Endowment) is preparing a report that will cover, among other fields, instruction and curricula in history and social science.

minority-group leadership, to hypothesis-testing in the social sciences.

SRSS's second undertaking is to produce a one-semester sociology course for the eleventh or twelfth grade. Like the "episodes" above, this course has been written by teams of sociologists and high school teachers. Both the episodes and the course emphasize inductive learning. There are numerous exercises in which the students have to deal with data. Tests show that this is of great interest to high school students, and that the exercises are valuable learning devices.

In a third effort, SRSS is putting out a series of six paperback books for supplementary reading. The first two of these are *Cities and City Life* and *Life in Families*. Others are planned on race relations, the population explosion, delinquency and crime, and bureaucracy. Each book is to be made up of eighteen to twenty authoritative monographs or research articles by sociologists, that have been completely rewritten by freelance authors employed by the project.

The Commission notes that a substantial portion of the recent effort to strengthen the social sciences has centered on the problem of interdisciplinary integration, simply because there is not room in a crowded curriculum for each discipline to have its place in the sun. While an introduction to the social science disciplines per se ought to be available some time during the twelve-year sequence, it just does not appear feasible to fit full disciplinary coverage into the one-hour-a-day available on the average for all the social studies. The implication is clear. Each discipline will sooner or later be forced to ask itself: (1) What learning objectives deserve a place in the curriculum? (2) In what sequences can they be most readily learned? Such focusing of attention on objectives may, perhaps, minimize the rivalry among the social sciences for a place in the curriculum.

The Commission recommends that the National Science Foundation (1) continue and increase its support of social science curriculum development for elementary and secondary schools, and (2) encourage the presently inactive social science associations to take responsibility for developing such curriculum materials. We further recommend that joint planning be undertaken to develop a social science curriculum that can realistically be encompassed in a school's program, given the constraints of competition for time from other fields of knowledge. Such joint planning should involve representatives of most, if not all, social science and social studies associations. We further recommend that more effective liaison be established among associations, the National Council for the Social Studies, and the curriculum-development efforts of other special groups.

2. *Research base for the social science curriculum.* Development of social science courses should be based on knowledge of the intellectual development of American youth. Again we find organizations such as the National Council for the Social Studies engaged in research efforts in this area. These studies, in the main, focus on six issues: comparative content; the impact of social change on the curriculum; types of concepts learned from different curricula; methods of instruction; methods of evaluation; and teacher training.[4]

A very promising effort by social scientists is now developing, based on child development research, to examine how children of different ages learn key social science concepts.

The earliest efforts of this type came from psychology, with special reference to the child's development of concepts of motivation and of group norms. The work of Ralph H. Ojemann of the State University of Iowa is exemplary in this respect.[5] More recently, political scientists have studied the acquisition and development of political and social concepts and the implications of these for the political system as well as for the social studies curriculum.[6]

Two major strands of empirical research are apparent thus far. (1) The *developmental approach,* which places great weight on the unfolding of value acquisition as the child matures. Longitudinal and quasi-longitudinal study designs are fruitful approaches here, although virtually only the latter has been so far exploited. (2) The empirical work has focused more on the *source* or *agent-phenomena approach,* which directs attention to the conditions under which the child acquires certain orientations, and the relative and differential contributions of these conditions at different stages in the child's growth. Either static or time-series studies are appropriate; and the former has so far predominated.

Such research into what the young learn, how they learn, and with what effects is clearly relevant for such diverse fields as race

---

[4] See Benjamin C. Cox, William D. Johnson, and Roland F. Payette, "Review of Research in Social Studies: 1967," *Social Education,* XXXII (October, 1968).
[5] See Ralph H. Ojemann (ed.), *Four Basic Aspects of Preventive Psychiatry:* Report of the First Institute on Preventive Psychiatry (Iowa City: State University of Iowa, 1957), Chap. IV. See also Barbara Ellis Long, "Teaching Psychology to Children," *American Psychologist,* 23 (September, 1968), 691–692; John J. Patrick, *Political Socialization of American Youth* (for a review of the research on political socialization), Research Bulletin No. 3 (Washington, D.C.: National Council for the Social Studies, 1967).
[6] Kenneth P. Langton and M. Kent Jennings, "Political Socialization and the High School Civics Curriculum in the United States," *The American Political Science Review,* LXII (September, 1968). See also the special issue on political socialization of the *Harvard Educational Review,* 38 (1968).

and intergroup relations; problems of alienation, cynicism, and despair; participative orientations among mass publics; normative conceptions of the good society; international conflict and cooperation; the training and preparation of teachers; the content of the mass media; and community-action programs involving youth.

Nowhere, perhaps, are the implications more apparent than in the educational system. This is so in our society because schools are primarily public institutions and thus considered "legitimate" channels through which to achieve socially desired ends—in contrast, for example, to the fierce constraints felt in this country against any outside interference with family life. So much of a child's life is spent in the school environment that it may well exert undue influence on the political socialization of youth. The school supplies much of the child's social and peer group experiences in addition to the formal and informal curriculum.

In the light of this, we strongly recommend that social science associations and funding organizations encourage the efforts of scholars studying how children develop an understanding of basic social science concepts; and that special attention be given to the implications of this research for redesigning the elementary school social science curriculum.

Adult Education

The Commission believes that two important objectives should be stressed here: (1) to develop further adult educational programs in the social sciences, and (2) to involve the mass media in similar informal efforts.

1. *Formal educational programs.* The range of formal adult education in the United States today is extremely wide.[7] Almost thirty million people report themselves as taking part in some kind of adult education course or activity, as shown in a 1961–1962 survey by the National Opinion Research Center.

Participation, however, is unequally distributed among different groups in the American population. It is mostly the younger group of adults (under forty years of age) rather than the older adults (over forty years of age) who are so engaged. There are about equal numbers of men and women and, it is important to note, *no* significant differences in religious background or in race. The clearest distinguishing characteristic of those participating in adult education is that they are already among the best educated. In the data

---

[7] See J. M. Ziegler, "Continuing Education in the University," *Daedalus*, 93 (Fall, 1964), 1162–1183. See also Steven Goodman, *National Directory of Adult and Continuing Education* (Rochester, N.Y.: Educational Training Association, 1968).

reported, only 4 per cent with no schooling sought adult education, while 47 per cent of those with more than sixteen years of schooling sought more. These figures suggest that a given amount of education may be a threshold over which one must cross—both to awaken interest in self-growth and self-improvement leading to self-initiated adult socialization, and also to reach occupational levels where the job demands are for continuing updating of one's occupation skills.

Important adult education in the social sciences also takes place in special seminars and conferences designed to bring national and community leaders into discussion with social scientists. The advanced study program—of which the Urban Policy Conferences are a part—of The Brookings Institution provides a good illustration.

Brookings convenes these conferences to organize and transform the new information from urban research into the intelligence needed for informed policy-making in urban affairs. The information to be presented is identified and organized beforehand by The Brookings Institution, in association with the major centers of research in the United States and abroad.

> An Urban Policy Conference can consider theories, projects, programs, problems, and policies related to urban affairs. Conceivably, a Conference could consider the construction of a building, a resolution of a civic dispute, a community renewal program, a manpower policy, a master plan, a research report, or suggest research design.
>
> Such a policy planning Conference can be composed of public officials, elected or appointed, of executives of civic institutions, or heads of utility systems, of business executives, of corporation presidents, of representatives of professional groups, indeed of those civic leaders with public responsibilities, or of any citizens' group, so long as it is concerned with urban policy.[8]

The Commission recommends, on the basis of the foregoing premises and facts, that steps be taken to increase the amount of social science content in formal continuing education programs in this country, and that more special seminar and conference programs, which bring together community leaders and social scientists, be instituted. The fact that many of the continuing education programs in this country (exclusive of continuing professional education) are university supported, and expected to be on a self-sustaining basis, means that funds usually are not available for experimental and developmental program work.

Specifically, more funds should be assigned to the Division of

---

[8] John Osman, "A Model of the Urban Policy Conference" (mineographed; Washington, D.C.: The Brookings Institution, 1968), 1.

Adult Education of the Office of Education so that it can add professional and technical staff to develop the social science component of the continuing education programs that it now supports; and further funds should be added to implement the programs thus developed. In addition, consideration should be given to launching new federal efforts in continuing education through other appropriate agencies, perhaps the National Science Foundation or the National Endowment for the Humanities. Grants to continuing education organizations, primarily university-based but not solely so, should be made to enable these organizations to develop further their work in the social sciences.

Second, appropriate government agencies, and especially private foundations, should encourage the expansion of special seminar and conference programs and provide appropriate funding for these, to bring together social scientists and community leaders in policy-oriented discussion of social problems.

2. *The mass media.* The mass media provide another effective means for educating the public about the social sciences. Earlier we discussed the profession of journalism, and the contributions social science can make to broadening the resources of this profession in reporting and interpreting events in our society. Now we are concerned with something different—the mass-media reporting and dissemination of social science knowledge to the public.

In television programing, occasionally, there are excellent commercial-channel programs or documentaries which draw on the social sciences—for example, the CBS series on "Black America" and the ABC report on Africa. But the responsibility for educational programing with any significant social science content has usually fallen on the nonprofit sector of the industry, which has done excellent work considering the burden of its financial problems. Television programing presents a large and unrealized opportunity for social science education of the general public.

A good illustration of the kind of program that should be developed and presented in greater numbers is a program of the National Education Television network shown several years ago. This particular program was devoted to the population problem, and was prepared in collaboration with the Population Council. A national survey sponsored by the Population Council revealed areas of substantial misinformation, or simple lack of information, about the facts descriptive of this country's population and the serious social issues involved. Accordingly, educational films were prepared and presented through the National Education Television network throughout the country. These films are still available from the Audio-Visual Center, Indiana University, and have, since their first showing, been used substantially on a sale-and-rental basis to American schools.

The Commission believes it highly desirable for the commercial networks to produce programs with significant social science content more frequently. These networks have demonstrated that they can do so at high levels of excellence—they should do so as part of their growing responsibility to the public. In future productions of such documentaries or series, we recommend to the networks that they establish panels of social science consultants to provide more systematic and authoritative social science content.

With respect to nonprofit television, the Commission has the following recommendations to make. As increased funding for the Corporation for Public Broadcasting develops, provision should be made for professional and technical staffing. This staff would be responsible for a social science planning unit that could provide resources for program development in educational television. Furthermore, if funding of the agency carries with it any earmarking of funds for coverage of special areas, we recommend strongly that the social sciences be included. The establishment of a major nonprofit center or institute (with a staff including both social scientists and journalists) should also be considered—to produce distinguished social science documentaries for use in television programing.

There are few instances in which newspaper journalists achieved distinction in the social sciences, or in which social scientists attained success in journalism. Robert E. Park left an established career as a newspaper and magazine writer to become one of the outstanding sociologists of his day; Walter Lippmann, already known as a brilliant political scientist, rapidly emerged as a luminary of political journalism; such well-known economists as J. K. Galbraith are at home in both the mass media and the universities; and a number of recognized psychologists and psychiatrists have regularly written for the press during the past decades—but these are exceptions. Only in the field of economics have the mass media developed a small corps of expert writers and commentators who devote themselves to keeping abreast of economic research and thinking, and who write with authority.

The greatest single advance—and the one most difficult to achieve—would be recognition by policy-makers in the news industry that journalists specializing in the social sciences deserve their moral and financial support. Race, crime, drugs, the family, and even politics can no longer be covered satisfactorily by the generalist. The industry has recognized this in the case of economics, and it is now the time to develop specialists in other areas of the social sciences as well. The Commission recommends that the newspaper industry accept the concept of a "social science beat" and develop specialists on their staffs in the social sciences.

Magazine and book writers have made important contributions to public education in the social sciences. There is a long history, almost coextensive with social science in this nation, of reporting of social science to public audiences through magazine articles and popular books. Both the audiences for magazine and book treatment of social science materials seem to be rapidly growing ones. New magazines devoted to popular reporting of the social sciences have appeared in the last few years, and well-known magazines of long standing have initiated departments on social science news. A recent popular book on sleep and dreaming is an excellent model for the translation of scientific research for public interest, as are books on the population problem, drug addiction, child development, analyses of the political process, to name a few among the number of noteworthy popular reports.

Much more can be done to promote the role of the freelance writer in social science reporting through books and magazine articles. In some instances the writer would be reporting on a major program of social science research such as the work of a given institute, and in such cases it would help for the writer to be brought in early to witness the planning and execution of the research program. In other instances, the writer may summarize a field of research, reporting the contributions of many scientists and research centers.

To further the dissemination of advances in social science knowledge and to speed their utilization, the Commission recommends that, where possible, research program directors and research institutes engage writers for the purpose of preparing articles and books for a public audience. The Commission recommends also that research funding organizations consider the desirability of providing a portion of the grant funds for the employment of writers for this purpose. The Commission further recommends that funding organizations, and especially the private foundations, view with favor proposals from freelance writers for the translation of social science research for lay audiences.

VIII

SOCIAL PROBLEM

RESEARCH

INSTITUTES

The Commission believes that engaging the best of our social science resources to meet contemporary social problems requires the establishment of a new kind of institute with the clearly defined purpose of carrying on applied social science research on problems of public significance. The Commission proposes the formation of special social problem research institutes where social problems will be analyzed by teams of specialists from the social sciences and other sciences and professions. Engineers and other professionals must join with social scientists in these efforts. Their technical knowledge is indispensable to any analysis of causes of and solutions to various social problems. Furthermore, each institute must establish close relationships with the agencies or organizations faced with the problem and responsible for its solution at the policy and action level, so that the implication of the institute's studies can be carried forward to the development of policy alternatives and action programs.

In proposing the formation of social problem research institutes, the Commission seeks to change the management of applied social science. The present organization of social science research is not well oriented to attacks on national social issues. The Commission believes that the proposed institutes offer a reasonable hope for more rapid progress in the utilization of social science knowledge. New social problem research institutes will provide a means for implementing many of the recommendations made previously in the report, namely, increased collaboration between the social sciences and the professions, provision of social science knowledge to community organizations, liaisons with business and labor, and more effective transmission of social science information to government.

There have been a number of important attempts to develop this type of institute, and these have had an important influence on social science research and have led the way for the social problem research institutes recommended by the Commission. One can mention specifically the problem-oriented centers established by the Department of Health, Education, and Welfare, and by the Office of Education; and certain nongovernment centers focusing on violence and on manpower problems. Nevertheless, mobilization of social science for solutions to social problems customarily has been ineffective because the problems themselves do not fall solely within the traditional areas of a given social science. Instead, they require for their solution the collaborative focused efforts of the several social sciences, the professions, and other resource groups. The fact is that research conducted separately by members of one or another social science usually does not provide the necessary broad insights into the nature and resolution of a major social problem. With a few notable exceptions, the social research institutes in the nation have not been able to broaden their research programs to perform the duties the Commission assigns to the proposed social problem research institutes. The objectives of existing research centers frequently are the development of basic research in a discipline; that is, they are guided by the theoretical interests of the developing science rather than by the need for a solution of current social problems. Even those research centers with an applied social problem orientation customarily emphasize a single scientific discipline; or, their research clientele is business and the subject matter fundamentally related to a specific firm's concerns; or, when governmental, they tend to be either short-range in outlook or focused closely upon a specific agency's mission. Such research is valuable to its clients, and there is undoubtedly a genuine need to increase it, but it does not possess the interdisciplinary scope needed for the study of complex social problems. The proposed social problem research institutes will provide an essential missing element in the process of bringing social science research to fuller utilization at the policy-making and action level.

Pluralism is viewed as highly desirable. The Commission believes that many problem research institutes are needed so that each then can deal with a specific social problem and be organized more effectively than would be the case if a single institute were spread thinly over a wide variety of social concerns. Moreover, pluralism gives the opportunity for having several institutes whose subject matters and research projects overlap and thus provide the benefits of diversity and competition that are not likely to emerge from a single national institute. And, a larger number of sharply focused institutes means they can be established throughout the country— at universities and in urban centers as well as in the Washington area—which will add to the diversity of analyses, perspectives, and insights.

The Commission is convinced that an intensive research effort is necessary before sustained, effective approaches can be developed for meeting social problems. We would be remiss in our duty, however, if we failed to warn at the same time that the process may be long and expensive. Social problems that have persisted for generations will not yield easily. The costs of restructuring, restoring, or bypassing old social institutions or establishing new ones is especially costly. Interdisciplinary social research is a relatively new procedure, and many valuable methodologies remain to be discovered. But it is a necessary approach, and its utilization must be insisted upon. Significant sums of money must be appropriated for the institutes to assure that the program of research on social problems will be given sufficient initial momentum to keep it going despite the many disappointments and failures that will inevitably be encountered in the first few years.

Activities, Staff, and Location

Activities. A wide variety of social problems exists for study, but each social problem research institute should be established to concentrate on reasonably distinct subjects. Many problems are so highly interrelated that they require the attention of more than one institute. Some duplication of attention is inevitable as the problem areas defined by the institutes overlap. A partial list of social problem areas includes: urban transportation systems; violence; delivery of medical services; welfare and income-maintenance programs; urban government organization; crime, especially the problems of first offenders and juvenile courts; judicial systems and the provision of legal services; addiction (drugs, alcohol, and so on); urban housing; prevention of pollution of water and air.

Our intent is that only problems which are obvious candidates for interdisciplinary research—by social scientists and by individuals trained in other relevant sciences and professions—should be selected for study by the institutes. Specific operational tactics and research strategies are not at issue here, because institute directors and project leaders are the appropriate persons to decide these issues and fit the talents of their staffs to them. The project leader must, however, control his project and keep the staff members who are working on it in good communication with each other as work progresses.

Staff. Consider the various skills that would belong in an urban housing institute. They might include sociology, social psychology, anthropology, economics, finance, political science, management sciences and public administration, law, architecture, civil engineering, sanitary engineering, electrical engineering, medicine and public health, transportation, city planning, systems analysis, and statistics.

Each one of this multidisciplinary array of professional and technical skills obviously does not need to be represented by a full-time staff associate. Some skills may be satisfactorily supplied through consultant or other part-time employment arrangements; more than one skill may be provided satisfactorily by a single staff member. The essential requirements are (1) the availability of practitioners who are competent in the needed mix of skills, and (2) the full-time affiliation of those with the skills most important for the institute's research program.

The studies undertaken should range from the analytical stage through policy formulation to development of administratively operational programs. Specific research contracts may not require reports covering the whole gamut from analysis to programs, but each institute's research program will be incomplete to the extent it fails to generate continuing analyses and evaluations of the problem it has chosen and the policies and programs relevant to it. Similarly, the institutes must find successful ways—transferable in substance to other problems and other research staffs—to breach the disciplinary barriers presently obstructing collaborative interdisciplinary research in the social sciences. Such success is fundamental to genuine progress in the treatment or cure of social problems. The conceptual problems that are certain to emerge should stimulate important new developments in basic research.

Social problems have been subjected to analysis by scientists from one or more disciplines before, and few problems have escaped public or private efforts to solve them or at least ameliorate their impact upon society. It is essential that these institutes collect and scrutinize reports of such past and continuing efforts. This is not merely a question of maintaining a record of the past; valuable past contributions to knowledge must be utilized, and new efforts to solve problems must recognize why previous analyses and suggestions were passed over. Equally careful scrutiny should be directed to assessing past and current policy programs. In some respects, this will amount to maintaining a continuous program evaluation by an independent source, for feedback into the continuing process of problem analysis and policy development.

Considerable empirical research will be required for testing hypotheses, gathering data, building models and conducting experiments and pilot models of suggested policies. Statistical sampling and control techniques have been developed that permit scientifically valid social experiments, and institutes should be prepared to engage in such experiments as a constituent element of their research programs. Such sophisticated statistical and other empirical methodologies can be available to the institutes either by recruiting properly trained staff or by acquiring access to the skills through regular consultants. Resident staff trained in many of these skills must be recruited and the remainder made available on a supplementary basis by developing reliable consulting relationships. Subcontracting data collection should be encouraged, however, when existing organizations possess specialized capability for expensive work; for example, large-scale sample survey research. Similar considerations will lead the federal government to assume some of the statistical workload of the institutes after research has identified (and defined the concepts for) activities that should be monitored statistically on a continuing basis.

Location. The best locations for these problem research institutes would obviously combine the intellectual stimulation of universities, the contacts with policy-makers and administrators of Washington, state capitals, or major cities, and immersion in the locale of the problem. Equally obviously, such optimal locations are quite rare; most institutes will have to seek the best available mix of these characteristics in consideration of each institute's research perspective.

If the decision is made to locate an institute at a university, the question must be raised as to whether the institute should be an independent organization in the university locality, or part of the university structure (and, if the latter, how related to it). This is not an easily resolved choice. Past experience of interdisciplinary research institutes at universities is quite varied and sometimes discouraging; conversely, however, the universities are the major source of research personnel, and the staffing of an institute outside a university structure presents its own range of problems.

The organization of universities into departments based on academic disciplines fosters a limited focus—directed toward building their disciplines through the research of their faculty, and training students in the discipline's analytical procedures and techniques. University administrative structures and financial responsibilities are designed to foster disciplinary and departmental objectives. Departmental rewards—promotions and salary increases—can, therefore, be expected to be determined by the faculty members' contributions to these objectives.

If an interdisciplinary social problem research institute is to be introduced into the university structure, there must be some modification of present administrative arrangements. Research associates at institutes would use their original disciplinary training and keep abreast of theoretical and empirical developments in their fields; but the objectives of research at the interdisciplinary institutes would be the analysis of social problems and development of policy and program alternatives that can be implemented at the policy level. Thus, analytical contributions to knowledge within disciplines cannot be expected from such an institute's research activities; and if they do materialize, their importance to any one discipline may well be only secondary.

Accordingly, unless these institutes can be established by the top university administrators and boards of trustees as financially and administratively independent of the departmental structure, the Commission considers that the advantages to be hoped for from association with universities are not likely to develop. Research institutes would be able to attract the quality of people essential to their own difficult research objectives only when they could offer comparable financial rewards, security, and academic recognition to their staffs. The balance of skills needed in interdisciplinary research directed at solutions to social problems will not always coincide with the skills needed in academic departments; independent status would assure the institute's proper development. Academic titles, salary, and tenure structures should probably be extended to the institute's staff to assure that it has been given a *bona fide* place in the university—coupled with possible joint appointments in departments when mutual interests are recognized.

Development of this independence will eliminate conflicts of interest between departments and research institutes with respect to hiring policies. Departments seek a distribution of interests within each discipline that spans all its major subfields. Research institutes seek a balance that achieves a complementarity of research skills that will lead to progress toward research objectives.

Several universities are in the process of establishing graduate schools with programs that will lead to advanced degrees in the applied social sciences. Such developments will be instrumental in creating a hospitable environment for social problem research at universities. They are also encouraging from the standpoint of an implication embodied in these recommendations—that existence of the institutes will encourage universities to develop graduate programs training new generations of graduate students for careers in applied social research. Continued interest on the part of graduate students and their faculties in applied social science research is, of course, vital for the viability of the institutes and their research objectives.

Transfer of Knowledge—The "Client-Sponsors"

The research and development activities at the institutes will be of value only to the extent that they lead to action. Consequently, there must be close ties between the institutes and those with the power and responsibility to act upon their findings. Each institute, therefore, will have its "clients"—the individuals and organizations who use the institute's findings. These same individuals and organizations should also assist the institutes both in defining the problems (since the problems are theirs), and in obtaining resources with which to search for solutions—they should also be "sponsors." The "client-sponsor" can be defined, therefore, as that individual or organization which both uses the findings of an institute and also helps it to define its problems and obtain the resources to tackle them.

A variety of user relationships is clearly indicated: the best center of action for meeting certain problems is in the federal government; for other problems action must come from state and local governments; still others are the concerns of community groups, the professions, individuals, and private organizations. Moreover, some problem solutions will require new organizations to carry them forward. Therefore, the institutes will, in many cases, have to act as a catalyst for the creation of their own client-sponsors. Air pollution provides a good example. Pollution control will require innovations in social, economic, and physical technologies; and it will also require the creation of organizations with the proper scope and authority to implement the technological breakthroughs. Again, solutions to problems of crime may well require new organizational arrangements in addition to new research and development activities.

Certain problems are nationwide. Effective research and development work upon them would best be done by one or two centers working at a fundamental level. Yet the implementation of solutions might require action by many widely dispersed agencies. New relationships might be developed through professionals within the agencies, special "traveling" seminars, demonstrations, and through publications. In any event, a flow of trained manpower back and forth is essential to effective relationships between the institutes and their client-sponsors. Institutes must, therefore, devote resources to broad training activities—short courses, seminars, visiting professionals, and the training of students. This has the further value of producing, over time, greater numbers of qualified and experienced people to work on national social problems.

Funding

Current estimates of the costs of operating research institutes indicate a need for at least $50,000 per year in direct and other costs
for each senior research associate. This estimate calls for a median
expenditure of $750,000 per year for institutes with a senior staff
of from twelve to eighteen, and possibly as much as $5 million
for institutes with a staff of one hundred professionals. If we assume a median annual expenditure requirement of $2 million per
institute, and a population of twenty-five institutes, the aggregate
annual requirement reaches $50 million. Increasing operating
costs and salary levels will undoubtedly produce higher annual requirements in the future; any growth in the total research effort
will require even greater financial support.

Institutes should be funded through a mixture of endowments,
research contracts, and grants. The major source of funds will inevitably be the federal government—because of the magnitude of
the funds needed, because of the prior commitments of other
sources, and also because the federal government is now the chief
focus for action on social problems. Additional sources of financing are state and local governments, private foundations, and
private wealth (both individual and corporate). These sources cannot be expected to furnish more than supplementary support to the
level of the federal government's commitment; nevertheless, such
supplemental support is crucial.

The federal government in general avoids establishing endowments for research institutes. Its support takes the form of research grants or research contracts for specific projects that are
important to the contracting agency's mission. The National Science Foundation, the Office of Economic Opportunity, and the
Office of Education, among others, have set up research institutes
to which they have committed specified levels of annual support.
Commitments can be extended through the device of an annually
renewable five-year commitment—although these commitments
are always subject to the condition of "funds available." Commitments for full support are vital during an institute's first several
years of organization and recruiting.

In establishing social problem research institutes, the National
Science Foundation and all other sponsoring agencies should be
prepared to provide an institute with full support until it has established itself as a viable organization. After that time, NSF and
the other agencies may consider a reduction in the level of general
financial support in the belief that the institutes can compete in
the market for research contracts from mission-oriented agencies

(at all governmental levels) and from private sources of support. The objective of reducing the level of support is to provide some assurance that the activities of the institutes will be relevant to current social problems. A continued level of general, nonproject support will enable the institutes to continue various lines of historical, evaluative, and exploratory research that are not susceptible to funding by government agencies, and it will strengthen the position of institutes when negotiating about a prospective research contract with a mission-oriented agency. The fact that the institutes are not entirely dependent upon contracts nor entirely independent, will become a form of guarantee that the research contracts finally awarded reflect the best judgment of the mission-oriented agencies that must deal with the social problems and the respected evaluation of independent research specialists in that subject.

The Commission, therefore, recommends the following:

1. $10 million should be appropriated in fiscal year 1970 to the National Science Foundation for the establishment of social problem research institutes; this budget should increase in subsequent years as the institutes mature and to allow for increasing numbers, with an objective of about twenty-five institutes.

2. Firm commitments should be made to underwrite the full costs of the social problem research institutes during the first years of each institute's life; as soon as the institutes can compete for research support, firm commitments for funds should be reduced to 20 or 25 per cent of probable expenses.

3. In establishing these institutes by competition among interested universities and other organizations, the following criteria should be operative:

(a) a capable interdisciplinary professional staff that will concentrate its efforts on the chosen subject;

(b) the identification of appropriate client-sponsors, either within or outside the federal government, and a proposed way to communicate with and respond to the client-sponsor;

(c) the establishment of appropriate mechanisms to insure a flow of qualified and experienced people through the institute into the user agencies.

If it is apparent from the quality of the proposals for attack on a given social problem that effective resources cannot yet be mobilized in an institute form, the National Science Foundation should not feel constrained to establish an untimely institute. It should, however, explore each such field to learn the difficulties and obstacles, in the expectation that these may be removed.

U.S. GOVERNMENT PRINTING OFFICE : 1969 O—355-443